THE DECADES OF TWENTIETH-CENTURY AMERICA

AMERICA IN THE 1920s

EDMUND LINDOP with
MARGARET J. GOLDSTEIN

TFCB Twenty-First Century Books · Minneapolis

Twenty-First Century Books
A division of Lerner Publishing Group, Inc.
241 First Avenue North
Minneapolis, MN 55401 U.S.A.

Website address: www.lernerbooks.com

Library of Congress Cataloging-in-Publication Data

Lindop, Edmund.
America in the 1920s / by Edmund Lindop with Margaret J. Goldstein.
    p.   cm. — (The decades of twentieth-century America)
Includes bibliographical references and index.
ISBN 978–0–7613–2831–5 (lib. bdg. : alk. paper)
    1. United States—History—1919–1933—Juvenile literature. 2. Nineteen twenties—Juvenile literature. I. Goldstein, Margaret J. II. Title.
E784.L57 2010
973.914—dc22   2009000703

Manufactured in the United States of America
1 2 3 4 5 6 – VI – 15 14 13 12 11 10

CONTENTS ★★★★★★★★★★★★★★★★★★★★★

Crowds of people walk along a **BUSY STREET IN NEW YORK CITY IN 1920.**

FORWARD MOTION

The year was 1920—the start of a new decade—and Americans were focused inward. World War I (1914–1918; initially called the Great War) had recently ended in Europe. The United States had come late to the fight, in the spring of 1917. When U.S. soldiers were overseas, Americans enthusiastically supported the war effort. But once the war ended, many Americans wanted to wash their hands of world affairs. Despite hard lobbying by President Woodrow Wilson, Congress rejected U.S. membership in the League of Nations, a new international peacekeeping association. It seemed that Americans preferred to focus their energy closer to home—to the promises and problems of their own nation.

In 1920 those promises were great. New technology—automobiles, airplanes, and motion pictures—were transforming American life. For the first time, more Americans lived in towns and cities than on farms. The towns were small and homey. But the cities, especially New York and Chicago, were big and bustling. They were crowded with new immigrants, new skyscrapers, and new ideas.

Business was big and getting bigger in 1920. New products—toasters, vacuum cleaners, and refrigerators—arrived in neighborhood appliance stores. New cars rolled off the assembly line and then speeded down city streets. Even the music of 1920—the frenetic, brass-heavy jazz music

THE FLETCHER HENDERSON ORCHESTRA was a popular jazz band of the 1920s. A young trumpet player named Louis Armstrong *(back row, third from left)* joined in 1924.

coming from the nightclubs of New Orleans, Chicago, and New York—was fast. It provided a perfect sound track for a newly modern, machine-driven age.

A "new woman" was emerging too. Unlike her mother and grandmother, she did not need to can food and bake bread at home. She did not need to sew all her family's clothing. She could buy most of what her household needed at nearby grocery stores and department stores. Women of the older generation had covered themselves from chin to ankle in layers and layers of heavy clothing. The new woman revealed more skin. New fashions showed off her neck, her back, her arms, and her legs below the knee. And unlike women of earlier eras, the new American woman had political power. The Nineteenth Amendment to the U.S. Constitution gave full voting rights to women. Congress approved the amendment in 1919, and the states ratified it in 1920.

■ NOT SO FAST

Not everyone in the United States was on the fast track in 1920. Many people, especially small town and rural dwellers, were slower to embrace change. In many rural communities, most residents were white and Protestant. Their ancestors, many of them from Great Britain, had lived in the United States for generations. While adopting new technology such as cars and gasoline-powered farm machinery, rural dwellers also cherished the slow pace of country life. They valued home, church, and long-standing family traditions.

The nation's cities, by contrast, were filled with diversity. They were home to large numbers of African Americans, many of whom had arrived from the South during the war years. It was African Americans, in fact, who had brought jazz music to Chicago and other big cities. U.S. cities were also filled with immigrants from Russia, Poland, Hungary, Italy, and dozens of other countries. The newcomers spoke a myriad of languages. Some practiced Judaism. Many others were Catholics. They brought the clothing, cuisines, and customs of their native countries to their new homes in the United States. The cities also had universities, museums, music halls, and movie palaces. All this activity made U.S. cities a marketplace for new ideas about politics, art, and society.

The contrast between urban America and rural America quickly became a clash of cultures. For instance, many rural dwellers found jazz music jarring to their ears, even vulgar. Conservative on sexual matters, they thought the new woman showed too much skin. Devout Protestants, many rural residents were alarmed by the influx of Catholic and Jewish immigrants. Some of these

A Washington, D.C., park official measures to see whether a woman's bathing suit is shorter than allowed by the park's **1922 DECENCY RULE**. Such rules appeared across the country in reaction to the revealing styles preferred by the new woman.

immigrants had radical ideas about politics and economics. Country dwellers (and a good many urban dwellers as well) saw these ideas as a threat to American democracy and business. For their part, many urban dwellers thought of country people as "hillbillies" and "yokels"—that is, backward, with their minds closed to new ideas.

■ HOW DRY I AM

With jazz music, new technology, the new woman, and the urban-rural split, 1920 promised to kick off an interesting decade. But one more factor transformed the decade from interesting to out-and-out fascinating. That factor was Prohibition—the ban on the manufacture, transportation, and sale of alcoholic beverages in the United States.

Prohibition officially began on January 16, 1920—almost exactly as the new decade began. But the movement for Prohibition had been building for decades.

Almost immediately after Prohibition went into effect in 1920, Americans began making liquor illegally. These law enforcement agents pose with **CAPTURED DISTILLING EQUIPMENT**.

> **"America was going on the greatest, gaudiest spree in history and there was going to be plenty to tell about it."**

—*Novelist F. Scott Fitzgerald, reflecting on the 1920s in a 1936 essay*

Since the mid-1800s, social reformers had expresssed strong disapproval of the evils of alcohol. They noted that some workingmen spent all their money on drink instead of caring for their families. They charged that saloons were gathering places for criminals, prostitutes, and corrupt politicians. They argued that alcohol destroyed people's health and undermined old-fashioned virtues such as hard work, honesty, and religious devotion. The solution, the reformers believed, was a nationwide ban on alcohol.

The movement for Prohibition picked up steam throughout the late 1800s and the early 1900s. One by one, states went dry, or banned liquor sales statewide. Finally, the Eighteenth Amendment to the U.S. Constitution outlawed alcohol nationwide. When the new law took effect at the opening bell of the 1920s, some people cheered and others fretted. Still others resolved to keep buying and selling liquor, whether it was legal or not.

Nobody knew exactly what the upcoming decade would bring, but with the combustible combination of bold women, big business, loud music, fast cars, and illegal liquor, anything was possible. Novelist F. Scott Fitzgerald marveled that "a fresh picture of life in America began to form before my eyes—America was going on the greatest, gaudiest spree in history and there was going to be plenty to tell about it."

9

OHIO SENATOR WARREN G. HARDING *(on train, fourth from left)* leaves Saint Paul, Minnesota, after a stop on his presidential campaign tour in 1920.

CHAPTER ONE

BACK TO NORMALCY:
1920s POLITICS

Warren G. Harding was not well known when he won the 1920 Republican nomination for president. An Ohio senator, he made the ticket as a compromise candidate after ten rounds of voting at the Republican National Convention in Chicago. The Republicans knew that Harding, although not their ideal candidate, was a loyal party man who would advance their big-business agenda. His Democratic opponent was Governor James Cox, also of Ohio.

Harding came from the small town of Marion, Ohio. He and his wife lived in a big wooden house with a welcoming front porch. This kind of house and the folksy, small-town setting were familiar to most Americans. Harding, a former newspaperman, seemed like an ordinary, plain-spoken guy. His campaign slogan was "Back to Normalcy."

■ FRONT-PORCH CAMPAIGN

The vague notion of "normalcy" appealed to voters. In the previous decade, the United States had endured a bloody world war—a mechanized war fought with new technology such as airplanes, machine guns, and even poison gas. Americans had also had to adjust to a new, speeded-up world of automobiles, electrical power, and assembly lines.

Most upsetting of all, to some, were the new ideas spreading across the nation. In big U.S. cities, some people promoted new ways of organizing business and society. They spoke about Socialism—a system in which government has strong control over business and the economy—and about Communism, an extreme form of Socialism. People who backed these systems believed they would lead to a more just society, in which wealth would be equally distributed among all people and in which the rich would not be able to exploit the poor. Other Americans talked about anarchy—the notion that all forms of government are an evil that must be destroyed. The anarchists envisioned a society in which people would live in small communal groups that would own land and businesses in common.

In 1917 revolutionaries had taken over Russia and set up a Communist government there. Some people in the United States wanted a similar revolution in the United States. Many of these "agitators" were new immigrants from Europe. Alarmed, the U.S. government had had hundreds of immigrants arrested and deported (sent back to their home countries) in the late 1910s. In 1919 the government imprisoned Eugene V. Debs, a Socialist Party presidential candidate, for speaking out against U.S. involvement in World War I.

IMMIGRANTS ARRESTED FOR POLITICAL RADICALISM arrive at Ellis Island in New York to be put on trial. The U.S. government successfully cracked down on those with radical political views in the 1920s.

" **Our supreme task is the resumption of our onward normal ways. We must strive for normalcy to reach stability. ”**

—*President Warren G. Harding, inaugural address, 1921*

In a speech in May 1920, then senator Harding assured listeners that radical ideas had no place in American life. He told voters, "America's present need is not heroics but helping, not nostrums [cure-alls] but normalcy, not revolution but restoration, not agitation but adjustment, not surgery but serenity." Carefully polishing his homespun image, Harding conducted his presidential campaign mostly from the front porch of his Marion home. He sat on the porch railing smoking cigars and jawing with reporters and visiting voters.

His opponent, James Cox, was by no means flashy or controversial. But as a Democrat, he was associated with the policies of the previous president, Woodrow Wilson. Wilson had won many critics with his post–World War I peace negotiations and his push to get the United States into the League of Nations.

Fed up with war, foreign ideas, and foreign affairs, voters overwhelmingly chose "small-town" Warren Harding and his running mate, Calvin Coolidge, to lead them for the next four years. The Republican ticket took more than 60 percent of the popular vote and 404 electoral votes to Cox's 127. Women, voting for the first time in 1920, overwhelmingly voted for Harding.

JAMES COX, shown around 1920, campaigned for president while he was governor of Ohio. His running mate was Franklin D. Roosevelt, who later made a successful campaign for the presidency.

TURNING POINT: Women Vote in 1920

WOMEN CAST THEIR VOTES FOR PRESIDENT at a polling place in New York City in 1920.

The Nineteenth Amendment to the Constitution, ratified in August 1920, states that the right to vote cannot be denied on account of sex. Ratification occurred in time for women to vote in the 1920 election in November.

Actually, many states had already granted voting rights to women. Wyoming had been the first. It had granted women the right to vote in 1869—before it was even a state. By 1920 fifteen states had granted full voting rights to women, and twelve others allowed women to vote in presidential elections. The Nineteenth Amendment required all states to grant full voting rights to women.

Earlier in 1920, at a convention of the National American Woman Suffrage Association, members had founded the League of Women Voters. The league was created to help the nation's female voters carry out their new responsibility as active participants in government. The league registered first-time voters, educated them about candidates and issues, and encouraged voting.

The league and other organizations did not have much time to prepare women for the 1920 presidential election. On Election Day in November, only about half of eligible female voters turned out at the polls. League founder Carrie Chapman Catt wrote, "Had the [right to] vote come earlier, more women would have voted and more women would have been trained for election work."

Still, Catt was pleased with women's first full participation in an election. She noted that several women had run for state and congressional offices, and some of them had won. She concluded, "The election is over; woman suffrage [voting] is here forever, and on the whole, women have good and sufficient reason to be fairly well satisfied with this their first participation in a great national contest."

After that first election, women registered and voted in larger numbers. During the 1929 presidential election, almost half of Americans casting ballots were women.

■ THE OHIO GANG

At his inauguration in the spring of 1921, Harding continued to hammer home his normalcy theme. He laid out his plans and policies, including lower taxes, reduced government spending, and less government interference with business. He once again condemned foreign alliances such as the League of Nations.

Americans were delighted. Woodrow Wilson had been a professor and a university president before entering politics. He had puzzled many Americans with his lofty ideals and big vocabulary. They preferred this new president, the golf-playing, cigar-smoking Warren Harding with his straight talk and commonsense ideas.

But Harding was the first to admit that he was over his head as president. "I can't make a damn thing out of this tax problem," he once told an aide. "I listen to one side and they seem right, and then, God! I talk to the other side and they seem just as right, and here I am where I started." On another occasion he told a reporter, "I don't know anything about this European stuff."

To assist him in governing, Harding surrounded himself with some capable and well-qualified cabinet members. They included Secretary of State Charles Evans Hughes, Treasury secretary Andrew Mellon, and Secretary of Commerce Herbert Hoover. But he also gave jobs to less capable men. Harry Daugherty, a longtime political operative from Ohio, became Harding's attorney general. Albert Fall, a New Mexico senator, became secretary of the interior. Both men were known more for backroom political deal making than for competent administration. Harding also filled many lower-level jobs with the Ohio Gang—his old friends and colleagues from Ohio.

Attorney General **HARRY DAUGHERTY** *(left)* was part of President Warren Harding's "Ohio Gang."

Harding's Ohio Gang soon earned a reputation for corruption. The president's pals took bribes, gave government jobs and contracts to their own friends and supporters, and did business with bootleggers (those dealing in illegal liquor). Harry Daugherty, the nation's highest law enforcement officer, was one of the most corrupt. As attorney general, Daugherty was accused of taking huge pay-offs from bootleggers and other lawbreakers and sneaking government funds into his own bank account.

Interior secretary Albert Fall orchestrated the biggest crime of the Harding presidency. He arranged to illegally lease government oil reserves—one in Elk Hills, California, and the other in Teapot Dome, Wyoming—to two private oil companies. In exchange, the companies paid Fall more than four hundred thousand dollars in cash and other property. When Congress began investigating, Fall resigned his position and went to work for one of the oil companies. The Teapot Dome scandal, as it became known, remained under investigation until 1929, when Fall was convicted, fined, and sentenced to a year in prison.

■ IMMIGRANTS

The urban-rural split widened during the Harding administration. In small towns such as Marion, Ohio, the residents were overwhelmingly white, Protestant, and descendants of northern Europeans. In Chicago, by contrast, almost one-third of residents had been born in a foreign country. More than one million Catholics—immigrants from Italy, Ireland, and elsewhere—lived in

Albert Fall *(left)* shakes hands with Edward L. Doheny, an oil company owner involved in the **TEAPOT DOME SCANDAL**. Fall was later found guilty of accepting a bribe from Doheny.

Chicago. The city was also home to 125,000 Jews. New York City had even more immigrants. Together they spoke more than thirty languages. Protestants were the minority.

A wide range of immigrants from all over the world had been coming to North America for hundreds of years. Employers particularly liked immigrants because they worked for low wages. But the majority of Anglo-Americans (those of British descent) looked with disdain at immigrants in big cities. Their dress was foreign, their languages were foreign, and their religions were foreign—and some of them clamored about Socialism and anarchy.

Nativism—the notion that native-born Americans were superior to immigrants—had increased steadily through the early 1900s. In the 1910s, many Americans called for stricter limits on immigration. Congress responded with literacy (reading and writing) tests to weed out poorly educated immigrants, as well as with deportations of foreign radicals.

By 1920 nativism was in full force. A nativist magazine called the *Menace* railed against foreigners, especially Catholics. The *Dearborn* (Michigan) *Independent*, published by automaker Henry Ford, attacked Jews. In late 1919 and early 1920, Attorney General Mitchell Palmer arrested and jailed thousands of suspected Communists and anarchists. The suspects included many immigrants, including well-known anarchists Emma Goldman and Alexander Berkman, who were deported to Russia.

Henry Ford's newspaper, the **DEARBORN INDEPENDENT**, regularly included attacks on Jews in its selection of articles.

Later in 1920, Italian American anarchists Nicola Sacco and Bartolomeo Vanzetti were arrested for murder. Because they were anarchists—and immigrants—
public opinion weighed heavily against them. "The jury [hated] us," Vanzetti explained. It was a "time when there was a hysteria of resentment and hate against
the people of our principles, against the foreigner." Although the evidence against
them was slim, they were both found guilty and sentenced to death.

In 1921 Congress passed a quota act. The law restricted yearly immigration
from any one country to 3 percent of its representation in the United States in
1910. In 1924 Congress strengthened the quota. It passed the National Origins
Act, which reduced immigration from any one country from 3 percent to 2 percent and based the percentage on the U.S. population of 1890 instead of 1910.

The new law ensured that most future immigrants would be from northern
Europe—places such as Scandinavia, Germany, and France—since in 1890, the
U.S. population had been largely northern European. The law severely limited
immigration from Russia and the nations of eastern and southern Europe—
since very few immigrants from these nations were living in the United States in
1890. The United States already prohibited immigration from China and many
other Asian nations. The 1924 law excluded Japanese immigrants as well.

Very few people protested against the new restrictions. Most immigrants—
having fled oppressive regimes in Europe and elsewhere—were happy to be
living in the United States. Most endured nativist taunts and slurs silently.

A boy sells pickles in front of a **JEWISH-OWNED GROCERY STORE** in New York City. In the early twentieth century, many Jewish people came to the United States to escape discrimination and violence in Russia and eastern Europe.

Most tried to fit in with their fellow citizens—to learn English and to become more like other Americans.

■ KLANSMEN

"Are you a native-born, white gentile [non-Jewish] American? Will you faithfully strive for the eternal maintenance of white supremacy?"

By answering yes to those questions, men became members of the Ku Klux Klan, a secret, nativist organization—dedicated to the supremacy of the white race and the repression of blacks, Jews, Catholics, and other minority Americans. The Klan had its peak between 1920 and 1925—with a top membership estimated at four million.

The Klan of the 1920s drew its membership largely from rural America—although many big cities had chapters. Members were white Protestants. By and large, they supported Prohibition and traditional religious values. Only men could be official Klan members, while women joined the auxiliary Women of the Klu Klux Klan. The Klan also ran children's auxiliaries.

Klan operations were shrouded in secrecy. Members met at night in remote outdoor locales. Sentries made sure that no outsiders saw the proceedings. Klansmen dressed in white robes and peaked hats, with masks covering their faces. They ended their nighttime gatherings with dramatic cross burnings. Klan leaders had magical-sounding titles, such as imperial wizard and grand dragon.

The Klan of the 1920s was a terror organization. It threatened, beat, and sometimes murdered those who challenged Anglo-American supremacy. The Klan's primary target was African Americans, but it also terrorized

Jews and Catholics. The Klan was also a political organization. It ran members for local, state, and national office. In many cities, it took control of local school boards. Once in office, Klansmen pushed an anti-immigrant, antiminority, pro-Protestant agenda.

The Klan reached its high-water mark on August 9, 1925, when about twenty-five thousand Klansmen and auxiliary members paraded in their robes, sixteen abreast, down Pennsylvania Avenue in Washington, D.C., the nation's capital. Shortly afterward, Klan membership began to decline. Its leadership was rocked by scandal and infighting. In some cities, groups formed to oppose the Klan. And with the 1924 National Origins Act having reduced immigration, the Klan could no longer stir up much anger about a foreign "menace." By 1927 Klan membership had fallen to about 350,000.

◼ SILENT CAL

On the evening of August 2, 1923, Vice President Calvin Coolidge was wrapping up a visit to his hometown of Plymouth Notch, Vermont. He and his wife had gone to bed early, preparing to leave the next morning. They slept at the home of Coolidge's father, John. Shortly after midnight, a messenger pounded on the Coolidges' door. "President Harding's dead!" shouted the messenger. "I have a telegram for the vice president."

The Coolidge home didn't have a telephone. The messenger had raced from the nearest telegram office, over narrow mountain roads, to bring the urgent news. Locating a phone in

Thousands of **KU KLUX KLAN** members parade through Washington, D.C., in August 1925.

town, Coolidge spoke with Secretary of State Charles Evans Hughes, who told him to have a government official swear him in as the new president of the United States. John Coolidge was a notary public, a state officer authorized to certify documents and swear oaths. By the light of a kerosene lantern, with Calvin's hand on an old family Bible, John Coolidge swore in his son as president in the parlor of his home.

As it turned out, John Coolidge was authorized to handle only state matters, so the swearing-in ceremony had to be repeated later in Washington, D.C. But the ceremony at the Coolidge home tugged at Americans' heartstrings. The scene in the family parlor showed that Calvin Coolidge was the quintessential small-town American.

Calvin Coolidge didn't smoke, drink, or gamble. He mostly wore a stony expression on his face and kept his words to a bare minimum. The press nicknamed him Silent Cal and joked that he could be silent in five languages. His demeanor was in stark contrast to the mood of the nation, which by then was in the thick of Jazz Age revelry, including much illegal drinking.

In this 1923 picture, newly sworn-in **PRESIDENT CALVIN COOLIDGE** wears a black armband as a sign of mourning for President Harding.

■ KEEP COOL WITH COOLIDGE

One of the first orders of business for the new president was cleaning up the scandals of the Harding administration. Coolidge appointed a committee to investigate the wrongdoing of Harry Daugherty, Albert Fall, and other lawbreakers. When investigations began, both Daugherty and Fall resigned their cabinet positions.

Progressive Party nominee **ROBERT LA FOLLETTE** gives his first radio address during the 1924 presidential campaign.

In governing, Coolidge largely continued Warren Harding's policies, especially promoting business growth. At a speech to newspaper editors in Washington, D.C., he stressed, "The chief business of the American people is business"—a quote that became famous and painted Coolidge as squarely probusiness. But he tempered that notion in the same speech by concluding, "We make no concealment of the fact that we want wealth, but there are many other things that we want very much more. We want peace and honor, and that charity which is so strong an element of all civilization. The chief ideal of the American people is idealism."

In 1924 the Republicans resoundingly nominated Coolidge as their presidential candidate. The Democrats nominated compromise candidate John W. Davis, a former lawyer, congressman, and ambassador.

" The chief business of the American people is business. "

—*President Calvin Coolidge, addressing Washington, D.C., newspaper editors, 1923*

The Progressive Party, a movement of farm, labor, and religious groups, nominated Robert La Follette, a senator from Wisconsin. Running on the slogan "Keep Cool with Coolidge," Coolidge won a landslide victory. His inauguration speech on March 4, 1925, was the first inaugural address ever broadcast on radio.

Coolidge's full term as president was undramatic. The nation was at peace. The Coolidge administration strengthened relations with China and Mexico and signed on to the Kellogg-Briand Pact, a multinational treaty that condemned war and called for peaceful means to settle international disputes. The U.S. economy grew strong during

Coolidge's administration. Employment figures rose, and businesses prospered. Prices on the U.S. stock market rose higher and higher.

Coolidge suffered a personal tragedy when his sixteen-year-old son Calvin Jr. died of blood poisoning in 1924. "When he [Calvin Jr.] went the power and the glory of the Presidency went with him," Coolidge later wrote in his autobiography. Coolidge privately decided not to run for president again in 1928 but kept this decision to himself.

■ THE HAPPY WARRIOR

The public was surprised in 1927 when Coolidge handed notes to reporters saying that he would not seek reelection. Instead, the Republicans nominated Commerce secretary Herbert Hoover. The Democrats put forth Al Smith, governor of New York.

Once again, the urban-rural split reverberated through U.S. society. Smith was Catholic. In his home city of New York, Catholics outnumbered people of other faiths. But across the nation, Catholics accounted for only 16 percent of the population. At best, Protestant Americans were wary of Catholics. At worst, they were out-and-out hostile toward them.

Protestant leaders warned that if Smith were elected president, he would take orders from the pope, the head of the Catholic Church in Rome, Italy. "He is likely to be tremendously influenced by the views of the Pope and the Romish [Roman] cardinals," stated Bishop James Cannon Jr., a leader of the U.S. Methodist Church.

Among big-city immigrants, Smith was very popular. He was a true New Yorker—

Democratic candidate **AL SMITH** was the first Catholic presidential candidate in U.S. history.

right down to his New York City accent (saying *woik* for *work* and *poissun* for *person*) and his campaign song, "The Sidewalks of New York." He opposed Prohibition, which was also unpopular in the cities. And his Catholic faith was a plus for big-city Catholic immigrants.

Once again, Protestant leaders bristled. Smith appealed to "the Italians, the Sicilians, the Poles and the Russian Jews," Bishop Cannon thundered. "That kind has given us a stomach-ache. We have been unable to assimilate such people in our national life, so we shut the door on them." The Ku Klux Klan made the most dramatic protest against Smith when it lit burning crosses ahead of his campaign train on its way into Oklahoma City, Oklahoma.

Fellow Democrat Franklin Roosevelt dubbed Smith the Happy Warrior for his upbeat disposition. Although Smith attracted enthusiastic crowds wherever he went, the anti-Catholic rhetoric hit home with the largely Protestant U.S. electorate. In November 1928, Herbert Hoover beat Smith by a huge margin. Hoover collected 444 electoral votes, while Smith took only 87.

Hoover took the reins of a prosperous, optimistic nation. At his inauguration on March 4, 1929, he proclaimed, "Ours is a land rich in resources . . . blessed with comfort and opportunity. In no nation are the fruits of accomplishment more secure. . . . I have no fears for the future of our country. It is bright with hope."

Chief Justice William H. Taft *(left)* administers the oath of office to **HERBERT HOOVER** *(right)* at his inauguration on March 4, 1929.

TURNING POINT: The Great Mississippi Flood

A TENT CITY IN MISSISSIPPI shelters residents left homeless by flooding of the Mississippi River in 1927.

The Mississippi River delta in the 1920s was a vast cotton empire. White landowners ran giant plantations. Both white and black families farmed the land. Most farm families were desperately poor, but events of 1927 multiplied their misery immensely.

In the spring of that year, heavy rains fell throughout the Mississippi River valley. Rivers and streams overflowed their banks. Along the Mississippi River, the U.S. Army Corps of Engineers had built levees, or embankments, to control the big river. As water poured in from tributaries, or feeder rivers, people feared that the levees would burst. Work crews buttressed the levees with thousands of sandbags.

On the morning of April 21, 1927, the levees gave way in several places. Massive swells of water flooded towns and cotton fields. The water uprooted trees and houses. It drowned livestock as well as humans. Survivors clung to rooftops and trees that remained standing. About one thousand people died, while seven hundred thousand others were left homeless. Downriver in New Orleans, people dynamited the levee on purpose—choosing to flood rural areas to save the city itself.

In Washington, D.C., President Coolidge seemed unmoved by the disaster. He refused to provide federal funds to aid flood victims. After considerable public outcry, Coolidge finally put Commerce secretary Herbert Hoover in charge of a committee to help flood victims. Hoover had earned his reputation heading post–World War I relief efforts in Europe, so he was prepared for the job. Hoover's team included six hundred boats, sixty airplanes, and thousands of people—nurses, National Guardsmen, and volunteers. Working with the Red Cross and private charities, Hoover moved 350,000 survivors into 150 tent cities. Like the rest of the U.S. South, the tent cities were segregated. That is, blacks and whites lived in separate camps.

Hoover wanted to lend money to flood victims, so they could buy their own land and start anew, but neither the Red Cross nor the U.S. government would fund his idea. The federal government improved flood control measures along the Mississippi following the flood but did little else. Herbert Hoover emerged from the crisis as a hero, which strengthened his reputation in the 1928 presidential campaign.

High-energy preacher BILLY SUNDAY was a leader in the fight for Prohibition. A former baseball player, he often raced back and forth across the stage and climbed on the podium.

CHAPTER TWO

THE NOBLE EXPERIMENT: PROHIBITION

On January 15, 1920, a strange funeral procession took place in Norfolk, Virginia. A horse-drawn carriage wheeled a 20-foot-long (6 meter) coffin to a grave. Actors dressed as devils and drunkards silently marched alongside the coffin. Ten thousand "mourners" cheered the death of "demon rum." Officiating was Billy Sunday, a fiery evangelical preacher and leader in the fight for Prohibition. The next day, Prohibition would officially begin. Sunday and others predicted that the ban on liquor would usher in a new era of health, happiness, and righteousness. He announced joyously:

> The reign of tears is over. The slums will soon only be a memory. We will turn our prisons into factories and our jails into storehouses and corncribs. Men will walk upright now, women will smile, and children will laugh. Hell will be forever for rent.

One day later, in the early morning hours of January 16, a truck carrying six armed men drove into a rail yard in Chicago. The masked gunmen tied up a night watchman and broke open the doors of two railroad cars. Inside were barrels of whiskey reserved for medical use. The gunmen loaded the whiskey into their truck and drove off. Their haul would fetch a hundred thousand dollars on the streets of Chicago.

Prohibition had officially begun. For the next thirteen years, Americans would be focused on liquor as never before. Some people would build up huge fortunes buying and selling illegal liquor. Government agents would try to hunt down the lawbreakers. Ordinary Americans would drink on the sly. Society would change profoundly—for better and for worse.

■ THE DRYS

Billy Sunday and other "drys" (those who favored Prohibition, as opposed to the "wets") had high hopes for Prohibition. They thought it would combat every vice: crime, gambling, prostitution, and government corruption. Henry Ford, who employed thousands of men in his auto plants, believed that Prohibition would create a more reliable workforce—since men wouldn't show up at work with hangovers. "With booze we can count on only two effective days work a week in the factory," he said. "I would not be able to build a car that will run 200,000 miles [321,800 kilome-ters] if booze were around, because I wouldn't have accurate workmen."

The Volstead Act, which set out the rules of Prohibition and enforcement, outlawed the sale, manufacture, and transportation of alcoholic beverages, but it did not outlaw drinking itself. People could drink liquor they had purchased before Prohibition. Religious groups could use wine for ceremonies. Doctors could prescribe alcohol to treat illnesses. It was not illegal to drink liquor in a private home.

The New York City police commissioner watches as **PROHIBITION AGENTS POUR LIQUOR INTO A SEWER** after a raid in the early 1920s.

The job of enforcing the Volstead Act fell to the U.S. Justice Department and specifically to Mabel Willebrandt, assistant U.S. attorney general from 1921 to 1929. Willebrandt was born in Kansas in 1889. During her childhood, her family moved several times to different towns in the Midwest. Her first job, at the age of seventeen, was teaching school in Michigan. By the age of twenty-two she was a school principal. By then she had moved to Los Angeles, California.

While working as a principal, Willebrandt attended college at the University of Southern California, earning both a bachelor's degree and a law degree. She became an assistant public defender in Los Angeles, specifically representing women arrested for prostitution. She also practiced law privately and got involved in Republican politics.

In 1921 Warren Harding brought her to work for the Justice Department—in part to appeal to newly enfranchised female voters. As assistant attorney general, she was the highest-ranking woman in the federal government. Willebrandt personally opposed

MABEL WILLEBRANDT had the tough job of trying to enforce Prohibition laws during most of the 1920s.

Prohibition, but her job duties included Prohibition enforcement, and she was determined to enforce the law. The work was frustrating because the Prohibition Bureau was understaffed, underfunded, and riddled with corruption. Nevertheless, Willebrandt managed to prosecute some big-time bootleggers, including Cincinnati's George Remus.

Willebrandt resigned from the Justice Department in 1929 and returned to practicing law. In the 1950s, she worked for Senator Joseph McCarthy, a vicious anti-Communist crusader. Willebrandt died of lung cancer in 1963.

29

When Prohibition began, saloons shut down. Breweries and distilleries also shut their doors or switched to making different kinds of beverages. Using hatchets to smash barrels, Prohibition enforcement agents dumped existing stocks of liquor into sewers.

Naturally, the consumption of alcohol quickly declined. Some people stopped drinking simply because liquor was scarce. Others did so because they did not

> **"No person shall manufacture, sell, barter, transport, import, export, deliver, furnish or possess any intoxicating liquor except as authorized in this act."**

—*Volstead Act, 1919*

want to break the law. Still others were teetotalers (nondrinkers) to begin with. In the first few years of Prohibition, hospitals and doctors reported fewer alcohol-related illnesses. Prohibition appeared to be working—at first.

■ THE REAL MCCOY

Then the bootleggers got organized. There was a vast amount of money to be made buying and selling liquor illegally. Much of the booze came from Canada, just across the U.S. border; from islands in the Caribbean Sea; and from Europe. Getting it into the United States required a network of boats and armed men.

Playing cat and mouse with the Coast Guard, rumrunners in speedboats smuggled booze across the Detroit River from Canada and from ships anchored off U.S. waters in the Atlantic and the Pacific oceans. According to legend, rumrunner Bill McCoy, based in the Bahamas, sold the highest-quality whiskey, in bottles wrapped in burlap sacks. Other smugglers copied his packaging and bragged that their stock was "the real McCoy," even when it wasn't.

Once booze was in the United States, bootleggers needed a network of clandestine warehouses, garages, trucks—and more armed men—to get the product to paying customers. In New York, mobsters such as Lucky Luciano, Dutch Schultz,

MEMBERS OF THE COAST GUARD CONFRONT A RUM-RUNNER on the Seneca River in New York about 1924.

LUCKY LUCIANO *(LEFT)* **AND DUTCH SCHULTZ** *(RIGHT)* were two of the most powerful mobsters in New York City in the 1920s. Luciano later had Schultz killed in a gangland turf war.

and Meyer Lansky controlled the liquor trade. In Chicago Al Capone was the kingpin. These and other gang leaders sold booze to illegal nightclubs called speakeasies and often ran their own speakeasies. The gangsters also operated brothels, gambling casinos, and other illegal businesses.

Vehicles and guns alone weren't enough to ensure the gangsters' success. They needed one more thing: corrupt government officials. To keep their illegal businesses running smoothly, bootleggers paid off cops, sheriffs, and judges. In Cincinnati nearly the entire police force was on the payroll of bootlegger George Remus. Overworked, underpaid Coast Guardsman and Prohibition enforcement agents were also quick to take bribes from the bootleggers.

■ GIN JOINTS

The Prohibition law presented a dilemma for many. Most Americans were law abiding, but they also saw little harm in enjoying a drink with friends. And with bootleggers supplying millions of gallons of liquor each year, those drinks weren't that hard to get.

New York "has more night clubs, cabarets and other such gilded dens [attractive hideouts] than hell itself," proclaimed newspaper columnist H. L. Mencken in 1926. In fact, the city had about five thousand speakeasies in 1922 and more than thirty thousand by 1927.

Bootlegging was not for lightweights. The mobsters who bought and sold liquor in big cities used machine-gun-wielding thugs to protect their lucrative trade. If one mob tried to muscle in on another's territory, the results were often death. In Chicago alone, nearly eight hundred gangsters died in shootouts with other gangsters during the thirteen years of Prohibition.

In Chicago Al Capone controlled the bootlegging business on the city's South Side, while George "Bugs" Moran controlled the North Side. The two men were sworn enemies. From his winter residence in Miami, Florida, Capone devised a plan to wipe out Moran and his men.

On February 13, 1929, a local liquor hijacker telephoned Moran. He arranged to drop off a shipment of stolen whiskey at Moran's headquarters, a garage on North Clark Street. What Moran didn't know was that Al Capone had orchestrated the hijacker's call.

The next morning—Valentine's Day—a police car pulled up to Moran's garage, where seven men were waiting for the hijacker's truck. Four or five armed men, two of them wearing police uniforms, emerged from the police car. The men weren't really police officers—they were members of Al Capone's gang.

When Moran's men saw the police uniforms, they cooperated peacefully. Bootleggers were used to the occasional police raid. They did not protest when the gunmen had them line up facing the wall and

AL CAPONE controlled an empire of liquor distilleries, speakeasies, gambling houses, and other illegal businesses in 1920s Chicago. He was behind the Saint Valentine's Day Massacre.

turn over their weapons. Then the gunmen opened fire, pumping at least fifteen bullets into each of the seven men. Six died immediately, and the seventh died a few hours later. Bugs Moran was not among the victims. He had spied the police car outside the garage and remained outside.

The Saint Valentine's Day Massacre made front-page headlines. Most everyone knew that Al Capone had been responsible, but police didn't have enough evidence to convict him. For many years, Americans had tolerated mobsters, even seeing the flashy Capone as something of a celebrity. But the brutal killings shined a new negative light on gangsterism. The Federal Bureau of Investigation joined the quest to bring Capone to justice. A federal jury convicted him of tax evasion in 1931.

THE COTTON CLUB in New York's Harlem neighborhood hosted some of the most famous musicians and entertainers of the 1920s.

Every night, New Yorkers flocked to the Stork Club, Twenty-One, the Cotton Club, Connie's Inn, and other clubs for jazz music, cabaret shows, and bootlegged liquor. Belle Livingston's Country Club on East Fifty-eighth Street charged a five-dollar entrance fee and forty dollars for a bottle of champagne. Whereas women had almost never entered pre-Prohibition saloons, speakeasies welcomed female customers.

The speakeasies were something of an open secret. They were hidden away in basements and down alleys. People had to give passwords or have personal connections to get in the door. But the clubs basically operated in plain view of the authorities. In fact, at Mary "Texas" Guinan's nightclub on West Forty-fifth Street, police and politicians were frequently among the patrons. The police regularly raided speakeasies, only to see them reopen under new names or in new locations. H. L. Mencken described the scenario:

But what of Prohibition! I can only say that Manhattan island seems to have forgotten it completely. One reads in the papers that this or that restaurant has been padlocked, but nine times out of ten it is open the same night, and magnificently wet. And if it remains closed, then its staff opens another and better one next door or across the street. Getting in is sometimes a bit complicated: one must be introduced. . . . Very respectable wines are procurable. The hard liquors are safe.

Supplementing the foreign imports, Americans also cooked vast amounts of home brew during Prohibition. "Bathtub gin"—a mixture of ethanol, glycerin, juniper berry juice, and water—was easiest to make. Gin and other home brews varied in taste and quality—some of it was even poisonous. To mask the taste of homemade spirits, people mixed in flavorings and sweeteners. The gimlet was a popular Prohibition-era cocktail that used lime juice to offset the taste of homemade gin.

Americans also found sneaky ways to tap into legal liquor supplies. Some people set up fake churches and synagogues (Jewish houses of worship) just to get supplies of sacramental wine. Doctors—happy to oblige paying patients—wrote thousands of prescriptions for whiskey as a remedy for "nerves." Across the nation, people bought liquor on the sly and kept hidden stashes. Many people drank from hip flasks. Some parents smuggled bottles inside baby carriages.

In 1923 a wealthy Boston dry named Delcevare King announced a contest to coin a new word. He wanted a name to describe people who brazenly ignored Prohibition laws. Two separate contestants had the same winning idea. They combined the words *scoff* (meaning "to mock") and *law* to create the noun *scofflaw*. The two winners divided the two-hundred-dollar prize between them.

■ SHOWDOWN

In some circles, people reveled in drink during Prohibition. Novelist F. Scott Fitzgerald wrote in *The Beautiful and Damned*, "When prohibition came . . . among those who could afford it, there was more drinking than ever before." Hollywood movies regularly showed people enjoying cocktails, even though it was against the law, and it was usually the movies' heroes and heroines who did the drinking.

A woman hides an **ANKLE FLASK** in her fashionable boot during Prohibition.

Members of the **WOMAN'S CHRISTIAN TEMPERANCE UNION** show their support for Prohibition in 1925.

But many Americans remained strictly sober and championed Prohibition, despite its obvious failings. Republican presidential candidate Herbert Hoover called Prohibition an experiment that was "noble in motive." Democratic candidate Al Smith, on the other hand, said that Prohibition was "entirely unsatisfactory to the great mass of our people."

Although Smith lost the 1928 election, his assessment was correct. By 1927 more than 75 percent of Americans favored repeal of Prohibition. Groups such as the Association Against the Prohibition Amendment, the Women's Organization for National Prohibition Reform, and the Moderation League attracted more and more members. Even so, the law remained in effect—and people continued drinking illegal liquor—until 1933, when the Twenty-first Amendment to the U.S. Constitution finally ended Prohibition.

Commuters crowd onto an "OPEN-TOP" BUS ON NEW YORK'S
FIFTH AVENUE in 1921.

CHAPTER THREE

MACHINE AGE:
TECHNOLOGY OF THE 1920s

The novel *Babbitt* by Sinclair Lewis follows the ups, downs, and ordeals of family man George Babbitt, a real estate broker in the midsized city of Zenith, Ohio. Babbitt has reason to be proud. He lives in Floral Heights, the best neighborhood in town. His home is fully wired for electricity and furnished with a full slate of electric appliances. Babbitt awakes in the morning to the sound of "the best of nationally advertised and quantitatively produced alarm-clocks, with all modern attachments, including cathedral chime, intermittent alarm, and a phosphorescent dial." When he goes out on the streets of Zenith, he observes a city in motion:

> All about him the city was hustling, for hustling's sake. Men in motors were hustling to pass one another in the hustling traffic. Men were hustling to catch trolleys, with another trolley a minute behind, and to leap from the trolleys, to gallop across the sidewalk, to hurl themselves into buildings, into hustling express elevators. Men in dairy lunches were hustling to gulp down the food which cooks had hustled to fry. Men in barber shops were snapping, "Jus' shave me once over. Gotta hustle."

Published in 1922, *Babbitt* exquisitely captured the mood of 1920s America. It was a nation on the go, with new technology providing the power and speed.

■ A-U-T-O

The car was still a fairly new invention in the 1920s. At the start of the decade, only about one family in three owned one. Henry Ford offered the lowest-price auto, a black, barebones Model T for the low price of $310. The Model T was topless, leaving riders exposed to the elements, and someone had to crank the engine by hand to get the car started. The car's top speed was 40 miles (64 km) per hour.

As the decade wore on, General Motors (GM), Chrysler, and other manufacturers introduced plusher models with hard tops, electric starters, windup windows, automatic windshield wipers, a choice of colors, and other improvements over the Model T. But they cost more—$510 for a Chevrolet, $965 for a Buick, and $2,985 for a Cadillac.

In the 1910s, buyers usually had to make a full cash payment to get a car. That changed in 1919 when General Motors introduced time purchase plans. A buyer could make a small down payment and then monthly payments (plus interest) until the car was paid in full. Other manufacturers followed suit, and by 1927, 60 percent of automobiles were sold on credit.

In 1927 the Ford company celebrated the production of the **FIFTEEN MILLIONTH FORD CAR**. This promotional photo shows *(from left to right)* the 1908, 1896, and 1927 versions of the Ford Model T.

In the 1920s, a decade of speed, auto manufacturer Walter Chrysler was always ahead of the pack. Born in 1875, he spent his childhood in Kansas, where his father worked for the Kansas Pacific Railroad. Chrysler followed his father's path and became a machinist's apprentice with the railroad. After becoming a certified machinist, he worked for various railroads in the West and Midwest, gradually working his way up to management positions.

At the 1905 Chicago Auto Show, Chrysler became fascinated with cars, which were still something of a novelty then. He bought an expensive car called a Locomobile Phaeton, which he disassembled and rebuilt several times to learn how it worked. In 1911 Chrysler switched from the railroad business to the growing automobile industry. He worked for Buick, a division of General Motors, and ended up as GM's executive vice president. Under his watch, the company grew into an automotive giant.

Chrysler left General Motors in 1920 and worked with several other auto manufacturers in the following few years. During this time, he and a team of designers created a car called the Chrysler Six. With its high-compression engine, four-wheel hydraulic brakes, and top speed of 75 miles (121 km) per hour, it was far superior to any other car on the market. With his namesake car, Chrysler finally created his namesake company, the Chrysler Corporation, in 1925.

WALTER CHRYSLER built his automotive empire in the 1920s.

39

Chrysler immediately became a major force in the auto market. In 1928 the company introduced its Plymouth and De Soto models. It also purchased the Dodge Brothers Corporation, along with its network of dealerships, foundries, and toolmaking shops.

In the late 1920s, Walter Chrysler sought a fitting headquarters for his automotive empire. He commissioned architect William Van Alen, to build the Chrysler Building in midtown Manhattan. For a short time (until the Empire State Building topped it), the ornate seventy-seven-story structure was the tallest building in the world. Chrysler died in 1940, but his auto company remained one of the "big three" automakers, along with Ford and General Motors, into the twenty-first century.

Auto companies advertised heavily, encouraging drivers to buy, and to trade in old models for newer, faster, and more stylish ones. "Gratifies your finer tastes, satisfies your every need," read an ad for the 1927 Oldsmobile Six DeLuxe Coach. Americans responded enthusiastically. By 1929, 80 percent of American families had cars.

Many roads were unpaved, although state and local governments had been paving roads steadily since cars arrived in the early 1900s. The federal government also set aside funds for road building. By the end of the 1920s, nearly 700,000 miles (1.1 million km) of U.S. roadways—more than one-fifth of all roads—had been paved.

One by one, states began to license drivers, register vehicles, and set up traffic lights, speed limits, and rules of the road. None of these efforts could fully prevent the hazards of car culture, such as traffic jams, drunken driving, and car crashes. Billboards and gas stations sprung up along roadways, while the Hertz Company offered its first rental cars in 1923. Overnight travelers could stay in "motor hotels," a term that the proprietors of a San Luis Obispo, California, outfit shortened to *motels* in 1925.

THE MOTEL INN in San Luis Obispo, California—built in 1925—was the first motel in the world.

By the mid-1920s, **TRAFFIC IN NEW YORK CITY'S TIMES SQUARE** was almost entirely cars and buses. The structure at right is an entrance to the city's subway system, which had opened in 1904 and expanded throughout the 1920s.

Cars changed the look of cities and streetscapes, and cars also changed social conventions. Young couples escaped in their cars to lovers' lanes after dark, much to the horror of their old-fashioned parents. Preachers reported that church attendance was slipping because families preferred a Sunday drive in the country to worship services.

Robert and Helen Lynd were sociologists who studied work, family life, and social trends in a typical American town, Muncie, Indiana, in the 1920s. When they explained their research to one resident, she exclaimed, "Why on earth do you need to study what's changing this country? I can tell you what's happening in just four letters: A-U-T-O!"

❝The rise and spread of the dollar-down-and-so-much-per plan extends credit for virtually everything—homes, $200 overstuffed living-room suites, electric washing machines, automobiles, fur coats, diamond rings.❞

—Robert and Helen Lynd, *Middletown*, 1929

Airplanes were still something of a novelty in the 1920s. The military had used them in World War I, and the U.S. government used them to carry mail, but passenger flights were rare. Most pilots were adventurers who tried to break records for speed and distance, or daredevils who thrilled crowds with their aerial stunts. In 1919 a New York businessman had offered a prize of twenty-five thousand dollars for the first pilot to fly solo, nonstop across the Atlantic Ocean. Several pilots attempted the flight, but none succeeded. Some attempts ended in death or injury.

Charles Lindbergh, a young airmail flyer on the Saint Louis to Chicago route, was determined to make the transatlantic flight. In 1926 he convinced a group of Saint Louis businessmen to finance the cost of a custom-built airplane, which he named the *Spirit of St. Louis*. Lindbergh tested the plane by flying from San Diego, California, to New York City in record time—twenty hours and twenty-one minutes.

On the morning of May 20, 1927, twenty-five-year-old Lindbergh took off from Roosevelt Field near New York City. He flew through storms, frigid air, and fog and struggled to stay awake through the night and following day. Thirty-three and a half hours and 3,600 miles (5,800 km) after takeoff, he landed at Le Bourget Field near Paris, France. A huge, cheering crowd gathered there to meet him.

President Coolidge sent a naval ship to

CHARLES LINDBERGH stands in front of the *Spirit of St. Louis* after his record-breaking transatlantic flight in 1927.

bring Lindbergh home from France. The ship arrived in New York City to a tremendous celebration. Two hundred other boats blared their horns in the harbor, and seventy-five airplanes flew overhead. Lindbergh then rode in a triumphant ticker-tape parade, with crowds of New Yorkers standing shoulder to shoulder to shout their adoration.

In the following months, Americans honored Lindbergh with more parades, poems, awards, and accolades. President Coolidge gave him the Distinguished Flying Cross, and Congress gave him the Medal of Honor—both military awards. For the rest of the 1920s, Lucky Lindy was the biggest celebrity in the United States—more popular than any athlete, movie star, or war hero. "Lindbergh is our Prince and our President combined," concluded humorist Will Rogers.

■ RADIOLA

November 2, 1920, was Election Day in the United States. People across the nation cast ballots and then waited to hear whether Warren Harding or James Cox had won the presidential election. Most Americans learned about election results in the newspaper the next day. But in Pittsburgh, Pennsylvania, if you owned a home-assembled receiver, you could listen to the returns on radio. Station KDKA, the first U.S. government–licensed radio station—operated by the Westinghouse Electric Company—broadcast election returns from 8 that evening to midnight.

After that first night, KDKA continued regular evening broadcasts of news and music. Westinghouse set up more stations in New Jersey, Massachusetts, and Illinois. Listeners were limited to those hobbyists who had put together their own radio receivers.

The Radio Corporation of America (RCA) was Westinghouse's rival in the radio business. It developed a radio receiver, the Radiola, which came preassembled. To increase sales of its product, RCA had to get more people excited about radio, so the company arranged to broadcast a much-anticipated heavyweight boxing championship between American Jack Dempsey and Frenchman Georges Carpentier. RCA set up a transmitter in New Jersey and installed receivers and loudspeakers in theaters, social clubs, and other venues all along the East Coast. Thousands of people gathered in the various locales to hear

THE RADIOLA RADIO was easy to operate and did not need to be assembled after purchase.

GUESTS LISTEN TO THE RADIO in a Washington, D.C., hotel in the mid-1920s. Atwater Kent, a radio manufacturer and producer of a popular radio show, stands next to the large radio cabinet.

the ringside announcer describe the action (Dempsey knocked out Carpentier in the fourth round). Excited, people rushed out to buy Radiolas.

Enthusiasm for radio swelled even further when Westinghouse broadcast the 1921 World Series between the New York Giants and the New York Yankees. By mid-1922, almost one hundred U.S. stations were broadcasting sports, news, and music.

Sales of Radiolas and other radios exploded, from $60 million in 1922 to $650 million in 1928. The early radios were large, because they held an antenna, vacuum tubes, a big battery, and other bulky components. RCA and other manufacturers hid all the equipment inside an ornate wooden cabinet, which looked like a nice piece of living room furniture.

■ "SELL THEM THEIR DREAMS"

With cars, radios, and various electrical devices, a new consumer culture had been born. And with credit purchasing, Americans didn't need all the money up front to buy a new washing machine, vacuum cleaner, or radio. Advertisers aggressively marketed the products of a newly electrified life to consumers. "Give her a *real* thrill this Christmas with a gift of a Frigidaire [refrigerator]," one magazine advertisement urged husbands. It added, "Use part of your Christmas savings to cover the first small payment."

Advertising, previously consisting of barebones business and product listings in local papers, became almost an art form in the 1920s. Experts such as public relations wizard Edward Bernays studied human psychology to determine which messages were most effective in getting consumers to part with their money. "Sell them their dreams," one advertising professional told his colleagues,

sell them what they longed for and hoped for. . . . Sell them hats by splashing sunlight across them. Sell them dreams—dreams of country clubs and proms and visions of what might happen if only. After all, people don't buy things to have them. . . . They buy hope—hope of what your merchandize might do for them.

Another agency executive explained that advertising needed to "arouse desires and stimulate wants, to make people dissatisfied with the old and out-of-date and by constant iteration [repetition] to send them to work harder to get the latest model—whether that model be an icebox or a rug or a new home."

Colorful magazine advertisements showed Americans enjoying the good life. "You find a *Road of Happiness* the day you drive a Buick" was a typical automobile ad. Conversely, advertisers warned that those who didn't buy a certain product—the right face cream, mouthwash, or hair tonic—would be doomed to social failure. Edna was "often a bridesmaid but never a bride," explained an ad for Listerine mouthwash, because her bad breath repelled potential husbands. The solution to this "pathetic" case was simple: Edna needed to buy Listerine.

This 1920s **ADVERTISEMENT FOR LISTERINE** says that Edna will never find a happy marriage if she doesn't use mouthwash.

This advertising photo shows **A FASHIONABLE WOMAN USING THE LATEST HOME TECHNOLOGY**, including an electric refrigerator and a home phone.

■ CARE AND FEEDING

Prior to the 1920s, people stored perishable food in iceboxes. These wooden cabinets had an insulated compartment that held a big block of ice and shelves for holding food. Naturally, the ice melted. So an iceman traveled from home to home in a horse-drawn truck to replace it. Homeowners kept a pan beneath the icebox to collect the meltwater.

Once again, new technology arrived in the 1920s. The electric refrigerator, which used chemicals instead of ice for cooling, offered many advantages over the icebox. It kept food cooler, resulting in less spoilage of perishable foods, and needed only to be plugged into the wall. No more ice deliveries or sloppy meltwater. In 1926 a Frigidaire home refrigerator cost more than three hundred dollars—a hefty price tag for a working family. Still, Americans bought refrigerators at a brisk pace, often on a payment plan.

Restaurants and grocery stores also installed refrigerators. Suppliers shipped perishable foods over long distances in refrigerated trucks and train cars. The American diet became increasingly varied, with spinach, lettuce, oranges, and carrots arriving year-round from sunny climes.

Meanwhile, manufacturers sold more and more brand-name foods, packaged in standardized boxes, bottles, cans, and wrappers. Wheaties cereal (called

"The Breakfast of Champions"), Popsicles, Gerber's baby foods, Peter Pan peanut butter, Fleer's bubble gum, and Baby Ruth, Mounds, Milky Way, and Butterfinger candy bars were just a few of the thousands of new packaged food products in the 1920s. "Mom and pop" grocery stores were common, but so were new chain grocers such as Piggly Wiggly, Kroger, and Ralphs. As more and more packaged foods arrived, women did less home canning and baking.

In part because of a more varied diet, Americans became healthier in the 1920s. In addition, scientists developed new treatments for diseases in that decade. Cities began regular street cleaning and garbage pickup, further reducing the spread of disease. School nurses taught children about germs and instructed them to bathe regularly, wash their hands before meals, and brush their teeth twice a day. More and more women had babies in the hospital instead of at home, leading to lower death rates for infants and mothers. These measures produced big results. In 1920 life expectancy in the United States was fifty-three years for men and fifty-four years for women. By 1930 the numbers had risen significantly, to fifty-eight and sixty-two years, respectively.

Residents walk past **GARBAGE DUMPED IN A PUBLIC PARK** in New York City in 1927. Before cities organized public garbage pickups, people often dumped refuse in the streets.

SKYSCRAPERS SOAR OVER NEW YORK CITY in 1929. The city saw the construction of the Channin Building *(left)*, the Chrysler Building *(center)*, the New York Daily News Building *(right)*, and other skyscrapers between 1928 and 1930.

CHAPTER FOUR

BOOM AND BUST:
THE 1920s ECONOMY

49

The United States began the 1920s in an economic slump. During World War I, industries had churned out millions of guns and other weapons. Farmers had shipped tons of grain overseas to supply armies and civilians in Europe. When the war ended, the business evaporated, and the nation endured several years of economic despair.

The bad times didn't last. In the early 1920s, manufacturing boomed, pulling the country back to prosperity. U.S. companies produced cars, radios, refrigerators, washing machines, electric irons, and other appliances at a dizzying pace. Businesses sprung up to advertise and sell new products such as Band-Aid sterile bandages and Kleenex tissues. By the time Calvin Coolidge became president in 1923, the economy was robust. Coolidge described the economic juggernaut in religious terms. "The man who builds a factory builds a temple. The man who works there worships there," he said.

Not only factories but also skyscrapers, bridges, and houses mushroomed across the national landscape. In New York City, construction went on nonstop. "In every block at least two new hotels or office buildings are under way," wrote H. L. Mencken in 1926. "For hours the pneumatic drills chatter and scream." Skyscrapers rose higher and higher—the Bank of the Manhattan Company Building (72 stories), the Chrysler Building (77 stories), and finally the Empire State Building (102 stories). "How long will it be

before office workers look down from their windows upon cloud banks," asked an editorial in the *New York Times*.

In what was called Coolidge Prosperity, the U.S. gross national product (the measure of all goods and services produced in the nation in one year) increased from $69 billion in 1921 to $93 billion in 1924. The unemployment rate fell during that same period from 11.7 percent to 5 percent and then fell even further to 3.7 percent in 1929. "We in America today are nearer to the final triumph over poverty than ever before in the history of any land," declared Herbert Hoover when he accepted the Republican presidential nomination in August 1928.

■ THE RANK AND FILE

The encouraging economic statistics did not reflect reality for many working-class Americans, however. Even though industrialists grew rich in the 1920s, the ordinary worker toiled for a low wage, usually six days a week. In this age of mechanization, factory workers were in some ways only cogs in the machinery. Visiting a Ford plant in the mid-1920s, Australian Hugh Grant Adams observed:

> At 8 A.M. the worker takes his place at the side of a narrow platform down the centre of which runs a great chain moving at the rate of a foot a minute. His tool is an electrically-driven riveter. As he stands, riveter poised, the half-built framework of the car passes slowly in

front of him. . . . Once, twice, he plunges the riveter down upon the hot metal . . . once, twice . . . once, twice . . . and so on for six, eight or ten hours, whatever the rule of the factory may be, day after day, year after year. . . . The chain never stops. The pace never varies. The man is part of the chain, the feeder and the slave of it.

In earlier decades, workers had formed unions to fight for higher pay, safer workplaces, and a shorter workday. But the union movement was weak in the 1920s. In 1919 and 1920, besides rooting out Socialists, anarchists, and other radicals, U.S. authorities had also arrested many labor leaders. Throughout the decade, business owners strived to keep unions weak and to keep workers from joining unions in the first place. Some businesses made employees agree not to join a union as a condition of their employment. Many businesses kept blacklists with the names of known union organizers and made sure that no one on the list got hired. Some companies hired spies to make sure employees weren't organizing in secret.

MEMBERS OF A MINE WORKERS UNION IN WEST VIRGINIA stand together during a protest in 1922. Miners endured some of the most brutal conditions of all U.S. laborers in the 1920s.

If workers still dared to strike (refuse to work) for higher pay and better working conditions, business owners treated them harshly, often bringing in strikebreakers to take over their jobs and sometimes hiring armed thugs to attack them. The Republican administrations of the 1920s were proudly probusiness and antilabor. In this climate, union membership declined dramatically, as did the number of strikes.

Not only factory workers but also mill workers, miners, and low-level office workers struggled through the 1920s. In 1929 the Bureau of Labor Statistics estimated that a family of four required a yearly income of $2,500 to maintain a "decent standard of living." Yet more than half of U.S. families lived on $1,500 or less. And if a worker were laid off or couldn't work due to illness or injury, the government offered no unemployment insurance or other benefits to help cushion the blow. Meanwhile, the rich grew richer.

◾ LEFT BEHIND

Farmers were also left out of the economic prosperity of the 1920s. Unlike the manufacturing sector, the agricultural sector never bounced back from the post–World War I slump. Through the course of the decade, crop prices sank steadily from their all-time highs of 1919. Farm families fell into poverty, and the companies that relied on their business—small-town banks, grocers, and hardware stores—hit hard times as well.

Two men stand with part of their harvest on **A COTTON FARM IN ARKANSAS AROUND 1925**. Cotton farmers suffered in the early 1920s as the price of cotton dropped.

TURNING POINT: The Florida Land Rush

Completed in 1920, **THE FLAMINGO HOTEL** was one of the first big hotels in Miami Beach, Florida.

As the 1920s economy surged, it seemed easy to get rich quick. Not only the stock market but also real estate beckoned the American with cash to invest. The hot place to buy was Florida, with its sunny weather and sandy beaches. In truth, Florida in the early 1900s was not all that enticing. The land was swampy and mosquito infested, with more alligators than people. But starting in the 1910s, developers set out to change the landscape. Around Miami, they built roads, planted trees, and drained swamps. Then they built hotels, homes, and golf courses. They advertised heavily in northern newspapers for new residents, land buyers, and tourists.

By 1922 the land rush was on. Thousands of Americans bought Florida lots and houses—not necessarily as their own residences but to resell when values rose, which they quickly did. As in the stock market, buyers often made a small down payment and borrowed the rest of the asking price. Miami's population swelled to more than one hundred thousand in the mid-1920s. After Los Angeles (home of the booming movie business), it was the fastest-growing city in the nation.

Along with a massive national advertising campaign, promoters lured northerners with a host of attractions: "bathing beauty" contests, alligator wrestling, and live entertainment. Architects gave Miami a distinctive look, with homes modeled after Spanish castles and Italian mansions. Meanwhile, property values continued to rise.

Trouble lurked behind the glitter, however. In late 1925, the stream of buyers dried up, leaving speculators unable to repay their loans, let alone reap big profits from their investments. In many cases, developers abandoned building projects partway through construction. Then, in September 1926, a hurricane hit Miami, flooding the city, snapping telephone poles, and knocking down homes and buildings. The damage was massive—four hundred people dead, sixty-three hundred injured, and fifty thousand left homeless. By the time another hurricane hit two years later, killing even more people, Florida fever was officially over.

A young woman stands with her suitcase on **A MIDWESTERN FARM IN THE EARLY 1920S**. As farming grew less profitable, many Americans moved to cities to find work.

Compounding the farmer's struggle, the typical U.S. farm family in the 1920s did not have conveniences such as vacuum cleaners and refrigerators. That's because more than 90 percent of farms had no electricity in the 1920s. Electric companies found it unprofitable to run power lines to far-flung farmsteads, scattered across miles and miles of countryside. So—just as their ancestors had—farm families made due with kerosene lamps after dark. They cooked food over woodstoves. Whereas most urban dwellers got clean, running water at the turn of the tap, only about 10 percent of farm families had running water. The rest hauled water from a well. Rather than flush toilets, they used outhouses.

In short, as the cities zoomed ahead, rural Americans lived much like their grandparents had in the nineteenth century. For farm families more than any other Americans, Coolidge Prosperity was nowhere in sight.

■ "THE DOW JONES COULD CLIMB TO HEAVEN"

A small fraction of Americans—about 2.5 percent—invested in stocks (shares in businesses) in the 1920s, and those investors saw big earnings. In 1924 the stock market began a steady upward climb. That year RCA stock cost $66.87 per share. By 1928 the price had hit $420, which made for handsome profits for those who bought low and sold high. General Electric and General Motors stocks saw similar big gains, while the Dow Jones Industrial Average—an average of thirty major industrial stocks—rose higher and higher. After studying the alignment of the planets, astrologist Evangeline Adams predicted in 1929, "The Dow Jones could climb to Heaven."

For many, the dollar signs were too numerous to overlook. Some people invested their life savings in stocks. Many banks invested all the money that depositors had left there for safe-keeping. Commonly, investors bought stocks on margin, or credit. They paid 10 or 20 percent of the stock price in cash and borrowed the rest from a broker. If the stock paid off, which most stocks did in those years, the investor could easily pay off the broker's loan and still see big profits. It seemed like a perfect formula for success, and as more people bought stocks, the market rose higher and higher.

A few people suspected that the boom could not last forever. Multimillionaire Joseph Kennedy (whose son John would become president of the United States in 1961) pulled his money out of the market in the summer of 1929. Financier Bernard Baruch advised his friend comedian Will Rogers to do the same. "You're sitting on a volcano," he warned. "Get away as far as you can."

Traders enter **THE NEW YORK STOCK EXCHANGE ON WALL STREET** in 1928.

■ "WALL STREET LAYS AN EGG"

The first sign of trouble came in August 1929. The Federal Reserve, the government agency that controls the nation's banking system, raised interest rates, the price that borrowers pay to lenders for the use of their money. The higher rates meant that it cost more to buy stocks on margin. With less easy money on hand, some investors cut back on their stock purchases. Fewer buyers translated into lower demand and falling stock prices, and a downward spiral began. As prices fell, more people started to sell their stocks, and prices fell even further.

Investors started to worry. They had risked their lifesavings in some cases. They owed money to brokers. What if stock prices continued to fall and they lost everything? The fear turned into a panic, and on October 29, 1929—Black Tuesday—the market came crashing down. Investors sold more than 16 million shares of stock that day. Some stocks that had sold for $115 earlier in the year were suddenly worth just $2 per share. In five hours of frantic selling, $10 billion vanished into thin air. Investors suddenly found themselves broke or millions of dollars in debt.

"Wall Street Lays an Egg," announced the show business newspaper *Variety* right after the crash. But the situation was no laughing matter. Even though

CUSTOMERS CROWD INTO A BANK TO WITHDRAW THEIR MONEY during the 1929 stock market crash. Panic about the crash caused many banks to collapse.

	1920s	2000s (first decade)
Average U.S. worker's income	$1,400	$35,000

TYPICAL PRICES

	1920s	2000s (first decade)
Chocolate bar	5¢	75¢
Bottle of soda pop	5¢	$1.39
Loaf of bread	10¢	$2.79
Adult movie ticket	25¢	$9.00
Pair of men's shoes	$7.00	$79.99
Child's bicycle	$30.00	$139.99
Washing machine	$112.00	$809.99
Passenger car	$1,500	$22,000
Three-bedroom house	$3,000	$300,000

(Prices are samples only. At any given time, prices vary by year, location, size, brand, and model.)

only a small percentage of Americans owned stocks, the crash reverberated through the entire U.S. economy. Some banks had invested all their depositors' money and then lost it all. People rushed to withdraw their savings but found that their banks were broke and had closed their doors.

Another downward spiral began. With their faith in banks and businesses shaken, people were afraid to spend money. As consumers cut back on their purchases, businesses lost profits. They had to lay off workers, which meant that even fewer people had money to spend. Meanwhile, the remaining banks had less money to lend to new businesses, which resulted in fewer new jobs.

The spree was over. The Roaring Twenties—as the decade was sometimes called—was no longer roaring. A new era—the Great Depression—had arrived. The last few months of the 1920s were marked by disbelief, anxiety, and fear of what might lie ahead.

This still from the 1924 silent film *Love's Wilderness* contrasts the decade's fashionable and flirty NEW WOMAN with a stern, old-fashioned woman.

CHAPTER FIVE

FUTURE AND PAST:
SOCIAL CHANGES IN THE 1920s

In 1924 a movie called *Alimony* hit U.S. movie screens. The film, involving a bitter divorce and the couple's eventual reconciliation, did not particularly stand out from the other romantic dramas of the 1920s. But no one could ignore the advertisement for the movie. It promised, "Brilliant men, beautiful jazz babies, champagne baths, midnight revels, petting parties in the purple dawn, all ending in one terrific smashing climax that makes you gasp."

Ten years earlier, such an advertisement would no doubt have shocked the moviegoing public. But by the mid-1920s, morals had loosened. Midnight revels—complete with jazz music, champagne, and petting (kissing and caressing)—took place nightly at the speakeasies of Manhattan. Instead of shocking, such activities were merely seen as exciting. Social norms had undergone tremendous changes in just a few years.

■ THE NEW WOMAN

Women's lives changed most of all. One need only compare the typical middle-class young woman of the 1920s to her mother as a young woman. In her youth, the mother wore a corset—a stiff, restrictive undergarment that squeezed her torso from bust to waist. Over this, she wore several layers of heavy clothing that covered her skin from neck to wrist to ankle. She probably grew her hair long and kept it piled

59

and pinned neatly atop her head. She wouldn't have dared smoke cigarettes and would never have been seen in a tavern—a rough, male-only hangout. Male suitors visited with her in the family parlor, under the watchful eyes of her parents. If she had a steady beau (boyfriend), the two of them had few opportunities for privacy.

Fast-forward just one generation to the young woman of the 1920s. Her clothing was nothing like her mother's. For one thing, the corset was gone. A bra, underpants, and silk stockings were all she needed for underwear. Over that, the young woman wore a silky dress or skirt that showed plenty of leg—everything below the knee. Her top probably had a low neckline. It might have been sleeveless or even backless. Her hair was cut in a boyish bob, her face done up with makeup.

Some older Americans saw this "new woman" as brazen, although the young woman thought of herself as fashionable. The press and pundits used a nickname coined during World War I to describe the short-haired, short-skirted young woman of the 1920s. They called her a flapper.

The flapper's attributes went far beyond physical appearance. If she lived in a big city, she might join her friends at a speakeasy after dark. There, she drank, smoked cigarettes, and did dances like the Charleston and the Black Bottom. If she had a date, the young man probably picked her up by car, and the couple drove off for an evening without chaperones.

A FLAPPER OF THE MID-1920s
wears a short skirt, silk stockings, and a cloche hat.

Contestants in **THE FIRST MISS AMERICA PAGEANT** line up for the "bathing revue" in Atlantic City, New Jersey, in 1921. Winning contestant Margaret Gorman is second from left.

Business owners in Atlantic City, New Jersey, were always looking for ways to attract tourists. Atlantic City was a popular seaside resort, but the stream of visitors died down after Labor Day every year. To keep them in town, in 1921 a local hotel owner cooked up the idea of a female beauty pageant, complete with a swimsuit competition.

The two-day Atlantic City Pageant, held in September, attracted only eight contestants. During the "bathing revue" portion of the contest, the young women paraded in typical bathing costumes of the era: skirted dresses with stockings. (Swimsuits that revealed too much skin were considered scandalous. Some towns even arrested women for wearing suits that showed their bare legs. Men's bathing suits of this era covered the chest.)

The winner of the contest was sixteen-year-old Margaret Gorman of Washington, D.C., dubbed "the most beautiful bathing girl in America" and later Miss America. The contest proved extremely popular, and Atlantic City decided to make it a yearly event.

61

But the changes went even further. A young woman of the mother's generation might have worked in a factory, school, or shop. But such a working woman was not the norm—and certainly not the ideal. Society dictated that women should marry young and work only at home—caring for their households, husbands, and children. In most cases, young women lived with their parents until they got married.

WOMEN WORK AT A SMALL APPLIANCE FACTORY in Newark, New Jersey, around 1925.

By the 1920s, the situation had changed. Society still preferred that women become homemakers. But economic necessity forced millions of women to take jobs. By 1929 more than one-quarter of all U.S. women and more than half of all single women were employed. Especially in cities, women worked in businesses that accompanied the booming industrial economy. They had jobs at banks, retail stores, law offices, advertising agencies, and newspapers. The poorest women, especially immigrants, did factory or domestic work. In all places of employment, women generally occupied the lowest-level positions. They earned far less than their male counterparts and had few opportunities for advancement.

But just having a job, even a low-paying one, gave women of the 1920s more freedom and independence than their mothers had had. They had their own spending money. Many lived on their own in apartments or boardinghouses. These women also had the right to vote—something their mothers did not enjoy at their age.

■ "YES SIR, THAT'S MY BABY"

The flapper had a male counterpart—a rakish young man who drove a fast car, parted his hair down the middle, and slicked it back with pomade. As pictured in movies and magazine illustrations, he also wore a raccoon coat and played the ukulele. The press occasionally called him the sheik (named for a 1921 film starring Hollywood heartthrob Rudolph Valentino), a label that never really caught on. Flappers and their boyfriends were based in reality but were also partially exaggerated by the media. Movies such as *Flaming Youth* and songs such as "A Dangerous Girl" might have signaled to some that the whole nation had fallen into a frenzy of immorality.

In reality, young people of the 1920s did test the limits. They came of age in a fast-paced, high-tech world, and they were excited to embrace new ideas. They peppered their speech with colorful

"Is the Younger Generation in Peril?"

—*Literary Digest* article linking rising hemlines to immorality, 1921

slang. For instance, if something was great, it was "the bee's knees" or "the cat's pajamas." Youngsters sneaked drinks from hip flasks and listened to jazz records. At the same time, parents, teachers, and preachers still held powerful sway in the 1920s, keeping the kids from veering too far out of control.

One area where young people pushed boundaries was sexuality. Employed and possibly living on her own in a big city, the single woman of the 1920s had more sexual freedom than her mother had had. Previously, social watchdogs had preached that sex was for procreation only and that women weren't even supposed to enjoy it. But the rules loosened in the 1920s. "After hundreds of years of mild complaisance to [acceptance of] wifely duties, modern women have awakened to the knowledge that they are sexual beings," claimed one sociological study.

RUDOLPH VALENTINO appears with Agnes Ayres in the 1921 film *The Sheik.*

MARGARET SANGER *(front left)* sits with her lawyers and the staff of one of her family planning clinics in a courtroom in New York City in 1929. She fought many legal battles to make birth control available to women around the world.

"And with this new insight the sex side of marriage has assumed sudden importance."

Thanks in large part to the work of crusader Margaret Sanger, some women—specifically wealthy and educated ones—gained legal access to birth control in the 1920s. The size of the typical U.S. family had been shrinking for several decades. The decrease speeded up in the 1920s, as more women were able to plan for and prevent pregnancies.

As women enjoyed more independence in the 1920s, divorce rates rose. Moralists fretted that the sacred American family was falling into ruin. But their fears were unfounded. Most traditional standards remained firmly in place. Whether or not she worked, the 1920s woman was still expected to put her husband and children first. Even the sexually adventurous women of the movies usually ended up, by the closing scene, happily settled into a secure, old-fashioned marriage.

■ OLD-TIME RELIGION

Americans of the 1920s were very skilled at blending old and new. They were quick to integrate old-fashioned ideas with newfangled technology. Consider, for instance, fundamentalist preacher Aimee Semple McPherson. She already drew big crowds to her 5,300-seat Angeles Temple in Los Angeles, where she offered a passionate religious message called the Foursquare Gospel. Wanting to reach a wider audience, in 1924 McPherson set up a radio station and broadcast her sermons to thousands more.

AIMEE SEMPLE MCPHERSON kneels to pray in New York in 1928. McPherson preached in person and also on the radio.

Radio was brand new at the time, and McPherson was one of the first to realize its potential.

New technology was one thing. But many Americans were slower to embrace new ideas in the 1920s. For instance, the idea of a new woman—one who drank, smoked, and worked outside the home—was shocking, even abhorrent, to some Americans. This new woman appeared to signal the destruction of all they held dear—home, family, and virtuous womanhood.

Rural areas were the most tradition-bound of all places in the United States. As Americans in the cities ca-roused in speakeasies, rural Americans held fast to the basics. Many of them went to church regularly and took the Bible literally—as the precise word of God.

In 1925 the Tennessee state legislature passed the Butler Act, which forbade teaching "any theory that denies the story of the divine creation of man as taught in the Bible." The law was specifically written to keep Tennessee schools from teaching the theory of evolution. This theory says, in part, that over millions of years, human beings evolved from other animals and that they share a common ancestor with chimpanzees, gorillas, and other apes. Since its introduction in the mid-1800s, the theory had appalled some religious fundamentalists, who held that God created humans about six thousand years ago, as described in the Bible.

Once again, the battle lines were drawn between old and new. Many scientists, educators, and journalists saw the Tennessee law as a big step backward for the United States. They believed that teachers should be able to discuss modern, scientific thought in their classrooms and should not be restricted to teaching ancient Bible stories.

65

Adversaries **CLARENCE DARROW** *(LEFT)* **AND WILLIAM JENNINGS BRYAN** *(RIGHT)* confer in the courtroom during the Scopes trial in Dayton, Tennessee, in 1925.

The American Civil Liberties Union, a group dedicated to defending Americans' rights and freedoms, wanted to contest the Tennessee law. It recruited biology teacher John Scopes, who agreed to be arrested for teaching the theory of evolution to his high school students in Dayton, Tennessee. Acclaimed lawyer Clarence Darrow signed on to defend Scopes. Fundamentalist and three-time presidential candidate William Jennings Bryan led the prosecution.

The Scopes trial became a national sensation. Reporters and photographers rushed to Dayton to cover the court proceedings. Because the theory of evolution held that humans shared a common ancestor with apes, H. L. Mencken, who covered the case for the *Baltimore Evening Sun*, dubbed the case the Monkey Trial. The streets of Dayton took on a carnival air, with hot dog vendors, musical acts, live chimpanzees in cages, and peddlers selling toy monkeys and other souvenirs.

The case was open and shut, since Scopes had indeed taught evolution in his classroom and had therefore violated Tennessee's law. But Clarence Darrow wanted to use the trial to make a point. He thought the antievolutionists were closed-minded—unwilling to look past the Bible for answers to hard questions. In an unexpected move, Darrow called William Jennings Bryan to the witness stand and grilled him about the plausibility of Bible stories such as Jonah and the Whale, the Tower of Babel, and Adam and Eve. Trying to defend the stories as accurate, Bryan became flustered and inarticulate. Darrow succeeded in making Bryan look foolish—and in painting the antievolutionists as ignorant and narrow-minded.

In the end, the Scopes trial resolved very little. John Scopes was found guilty and fined one hundred dollars. The Butler Act remained in place, other states passed similar laws, and the antievolutionist forces remained strong. Religious people denounced Clarence Darrow, while H. L. Mencken mocked William Jennings Bryan with snide remarks. Bryan himself died in his sleep five days after the trial ended. Meanwhile, back in the big cities, the forces of modernism continued to move forward. In rural areas such as Dayton, Tennessee, the champions of tradition continued to speak loud and clear. The United States remained locked in a battle between future and past.

■ SOUTH AND NORTH

African Americans of the 1920s were a people in transition. Like the rest of the United States, they were split along rural–urban lines. Most African Americans lived in the rural South, where their ancestors had once worked as slaves on cotton and tobacco plantations. Slavery had ended years before, but many blacks in the South lived not much better than slaves. Most were sharecroppers or tenant farmers. Under various arrangements, they

AFRICAN AMERICANS PICK COTTON ON A TEXAS FARM AROUND 1925. Most African American farmers in the South worked on someone else's land.

farmed a white man's land and paid a portion of their crops as rent. The system generally left African American farmers desperately poor and often in debt to their landlords. Their homes were nothing more than shacks. Their clothing was often ragged.

White southerners enforced a system of laws and customs to ensure that African Americans remained poor and powerless. Black children could not attend school with whites, nor could blacks eat at restaurants alongside white customers, shop in the same stores, or use the same public transportation. White government officials used a variety of legal and illegal tactics to make sure that African Americans did not attempt to vote, organize politically, or better themselves economically. The Ku Klux Klan backed up these tactics with terror, including the torching of African American homes and lynching, or murder by a mob. After suffering a beating, arson, or murder of a family member, African Americans had no recourse to legal justice, since in many towns, law enforcement officers were also members of the Klan.

To escape white terror, hundreds of thousands of blacks had left the South during the first two decades of the twentieth century. They had headed north to find jobs and freedom in big cities. By the 1920s, New York, Chicago, Detroit, and other northern cities had thriving African American communities.

Blacks in the North suffered less severe racism than their counterparts in the South. In the urban hodgepodge of many ethnic groups,

Members of an angry mob in the South surround an African American man during **A LYNCHING IN GEORGIA IN 1925**.

African Americans were just part of the mix. But racial prejudice still existed. In northern cities, many white employers wouldn't hire African Americans for professional, clerical, or even factory jobs. In many cases, a subservient position—shining shoes, carrying bags, or cleaning houses for white people—was the best one an African American could hope to get. Many white landlords wouldn't rent to black families, so they often crowded into grim, dark tenement (slum) buildings.

But racial injustice or not, the 1920s was a decade of progress and excitement, and African Americans were not to be left behind. In Harlem, a black neighborhood in New York City, African Americans ran restaurants, nightclubs, shops, newspapers, and other businesses. The community boasted a thriving art and literary scene called the Harlem Renaissance. Harlem also hosted a branch of the National Association for the Advancement of Colored People (NAACP), the nation's leading civil rights group.

THE NEW YORK NEIGHBORHOOD OF HARLEM was home to a vibrant African American culture of music, literature, and art.

1920s PROFILE: Marcus Garvey

In the 1920s, not many African Americans dared to challenge white authority. Marcus Garvey was an exception. Born on the Caribbean island of Jamaica in 1887, Garvey was determined to end the oppression of black people worldwide. He preached that people of African descent should return to their African homeland (which was then largely under European control) and reclaim it as their own home territory.

In 1914 Garvey founded the Universal Negro Improvement Association (UNIC) in Jamaica. In 1916 he moved the organization to New York, where it grew in size and strength. By 1920 Garvey had more than two million followers.

Garvey and the UNIC launched a number of businesses. They started a shipping line, with the intention of transporting blacks from the United States and elsewhere to colonize the western African nation of Liberia. Garvey also gave speeches to large crowds, published a newspaper called the *Negro World*, and crafted the Declaration of Rights of the Negro Peoples of the World.

The U.S. government was suspicious of Garvey and began investigating his business affairs in the early 1920s. He was arrested for mail fraud and served about three years in prison, from early 1925 to

MARCUS GARVEY worked as a printer and journalist before beginning his career as an activist for the rights of black people worldwide.

late 1927. After Garvey left prison, the U.S. government deported him to Jamaica. There, he continued his work on behalf of black unification until his death in 1940.

Garvey is remembered for his defiance and courage in an era when blacks rarely defied the existing white power structure. He served as a great influence to later U.S. civil rights leaders, including Martin Luther King Jr., and to the worldwide movement for black liberation.

Women dine at **A LUNCHROOM IN HARLEM IN 1928**. African Americans enjoyed much more freedom in New York and other big northern cities than they had in the rural South.

Chicago and other northern cities had equally thriving African American neighborhoods. Life in these neighborhoods was not perfect, but neither was it oppressive. African Americans, like most Americans of the 1920s, were optimistic about the future.

■ FORGOTTEN AMERICANS

One group of Americans in the 1920s had been nearly forgotten and badly treated. These were Native Americans, or Indians, whose ancestors—once numbering in the many millions—had been the original inhabitants of North America. In the process of settling the continent in earlier centuries, Anglo-Americans and others had wiped out millions of Native Americans. In many instances, the U.S. Army had slaughtered Native American warriors, families, and whole tribes. In other cases, diseases had swept through Native American communities, causing widespread death.

By the 1920s, the Native American population of the United States numbered only about 330,000. Most Native Americans lived on reservation lands in utter poverty. Some Native Americans had U.S. citizenship, which they obtained by serving in the U.S. military, marrying whites, or through other arrangements. But about one-third of Native Americans were not citizens of the land on which they and their ancestors had been born.

The U.S. government felt that Native American should assimilate into mainstream, white culture. White authorities sent many Native American children to boarding schools, where teachers forced students to give up their native dress, languages, and customs and act more like white Americans.

In 1911 a group of Native American professionals, many of them graduates of boarding schools, formed the Society of American Indians to fight for equal rights for Native Americans. The group was short-lived, shutting down in 1924. But that same year saw one big advance for Native Americans. Congress passed

Native American athlete **JIM THORPE** (pictured here in 1921) played professional football, baseball, and basketball. He got his start in athletic competitions at a boarding school.

PRESIDENT CALVIN COOLIDGE POSES WITH MEMBERS OF THE OSAGE TRIBE after the passage of the Indian Citizenship Act in 1924.

the Indian Citizenship Act, which granted U.S. citizenship to all Native Americans. After signing the law, President Coolidge posed for photographers with four Osage men, three of them dressed in traditional clothing.

The Indian Citizenship Act did not reduce poverty on reservations. It was only the beginning of a long struggle for Native American rights in the United States. For his part, President Coolidge won many admirers for signing the act. In 1927 he visited South Dakota and attended a Lakota tribal ceremony. There, Lakota leaders made the president an honorary chief and gave him a feathered headdress, which he donned for photographers.

Novelist F. SCOTT FITZGERALD AND HIS WIFE, ZELDA, dance the
Charleston with their daughter, Frances, at Christmas in 1925.

CHAPTER SIX

SCRIBES:
LITERATURE OF THE 1920s

During World War I, a young Princeton University graduate named Francis Scott Key Fitzgerald joined the U.S. Army. F. Scott or Scott Fitzgerald, as he called himself, had dreams of military glory, but he never shipped out overseas. At an army base in Montgomery, Alabama, he met and fell in love with vivacious Zelda Sayre. As he hung around the army barracks, he also began writing his first novel, *This Side of Paradise*. The book included a cast of characters much like Scott, Zelda, and their privileged circle of friends.

In 1920 *This Side of Paradise* was published, and Scott and Zelda got married. The two events coincided with the beginning of the exciting new decade. Perhaps no two people personified the glitter and irreverence of the 1920s as much as Scott and Zelda Fitzgerald. In fact, it was Scott Fitzgerald who coined the term "Jazz Age" with his short-story collection *Tales of the Jazz Age* (1922).

Fitzgerald's novels and short stories were populated by hard-drinking, high-living characters—wealthy young socialites, aimless college students, and bold new women. In his third and most famous novel, *The Great Gatsby* (1925), Fitzgerald turned a satiric eye on upper-class society and its quest for wealth and power. The book follows businessman Nick Carraway, the wealthy Jay Gatsby, and the enticing Daisy Buchanan as they seek love and money in the Jazz Age.

Fitzgerald was not the only writer who criticized U.S. society in the 1920s. Instead of mocking urban sophisticates, Sinclair Lewis brilliantly satirized the small-mindedness and pettiness of Middle Americans in his novels *Main Street* (1920) and *Babbitt* (1922).

Theodore Dreiser's *An American Tragedy* (1925) offered a disturbing view of Americans' obsession with wealth and status. The hero in this novel, torn between relationships with a lower-class woman and a high-class beauty—and intent upon getting ahead by whatever means necessary—turns to murder. Sherwood Anderson's novels and short stories of the 1910s and 1920s, starting with the story collection *Winesburg, Ohio* (1919), were keen dissections of small-town life in the United States.

Many writers of the 1920s rooted their works in specific regions of the United States. These regionalists included Willa Cather, who often wrote of her childhood in rural Nebraska. Set in the Southwest, *Death Comes for the Archbishop* of 1927 is considered one of Cather's finest works. The novel is based on the real life of Archbishop John-Baptiste Lamy, who ministered to the Hispanic, Native American, and Anglo-American people of New Mexico Territory in the mid-1800s.

Perhaps the greatest of the regionalists was William Faulkner, a southerner. In works such as *The Sound and the Fury* (1929), he chronicled families, both poor and rich, in his home state of Mississippi. Though often set in the fictional Yoknapatawpha County, Mississippi, his novels went beyond region and spoke to the nation as a whole.

Of all the writers of the 1920s, the poets were the least conventional. They embraced the new modern world by questioning established rules of poetic form. For instance, *The Waste Land* (1922) by T. S. Eliot was written in a fragmented, disjointed style, without standard rhythmic verses. The long poem was filled with allusions to myth and history. Many

In addition to writing books, **WILLA CATHER** worked as an editor and journalist. In 1923 she won the Pulitzer Prize for her book *One of Ours*.

readers found it confusing and off-putting. Poet e. e. cummings also attacked the norms and conventions of written language. He experimented with everything from the rules of grammar and punctuation to the typesetting of the printed page. He even wrote his own name with all lowercase letters.

■ THE LOST GENERATION

World War I had perhaps the biggest influence on U.S. writers of the 1920s. Although the United States did not enter the war until 1917, a year before it ended, the horrors and brutality of the conflict jolted Americans out of an innocent mind-set. The war had been fought with new mechanized equipment such as machine guns, tanks, submarines, and airplanes. This new technology inflicted heavy and gruesome casualties. Millions of soldiers died in the trenches of Europe during the four-year conflict.

A number of writers of the 1920s examined the war in novels. Examples include William Faulkner's *Soldiers' Pay* (1926) and the antiwar epic *Three Soldiers* (1921) by John Dos Passos. Ernest Hemingway, a young reporter from Oak Park, Illinois, and an avid sportsman, witnessed the horrors of the war up close. He worked as a volunteer ambulance driver in Italy, where he was badly wounded. His tragic novel *A Farewell to Arms* (1929) is a love story set in Italy during the war.

ERNEST HEMINGWAY *(front, third from right)* stands with the staff of an American Red Cross hospital in Milan, Italy, around 1918. Hemingway stayed at the hospital while recovering from war wounds. He set 1929's *A Farewell to Arms* in wartime Italy.

After the war, a large group of creative young Americans, unhappy with life in the money-hungry United States, moved to Europe to live and work, mostly in Paris, France. They were greeted there by Gertrude Stein, an avant-garde U.S. author and art collector who had been living in Paris for many years. Stein called the Americans in Paris the Lost Generation—meaning that they had lost the traditional values and attitudes of their artistic predecessors. These expatriate artists included many writers, including Sherwood Anderson, Scott Fitzgerald, and John Dos Passos. Most prominent of the Lost Generation was Hemingway, who wrote about his fellow expatriates in *The Sun Also Rises* (1926).

■ NEW YORK WITS

Writers who didn't join the Lost Generation in Paris found kindred spirits in big U.S. cities, especially New York. At the swank Algonquin Hotel in midtown Manhattan, a small group of writers and actors gathered for lunch nearly every day from 1919 to 1929. They sat around a big round table, where they exchanged jokes and witticisms. Algonquin Round Table members included columnist Franklin Pierce Adams, actor Robert Benchley, sportswriter Heywood Broun, playwright George S. Kaufman, writer Dorothy Parker, and Harold Ross, editor of the *New Yorker* magazine. Others moved in and out of the circle throughout the decade.

Perhaps the greatest humorists of the Jazz Age were two eccentric Midwesterners transplanted to New York City. From Niles, Michigan, came sports columnist and short-story writer Ring Lardner, best known for his satirical takes on the sports world, marriage, and the theater. James Thurber, from Columbus, Ohio, wrote humorous stories and drew cartoons. Many of his works (both written and visual) appeared in the *New Yorker*.

RING LARDNER wrote humorous stories and newspaper columns in the 1920s.

New York's Algonquin Round Table was also known as the Vicious Circle because of its members' biting wit. The ringleader and a cofounder of the group was the sharp-tongued Dorothy Parker.

Parker was born Dorothy Rothschild in New Jersey in 1893. Her mother died when she was four, and her father died when she was twenty. After education at a Catholic school, Parker moved to New York City, where she began a writing career. In 1916 she took an editorial job with *Vogue* magazine and then moved on to *Vanity Fair* as a theater critic. In 1919 she and writers Robert Benchley and Robert Sherwood began their daily Round Table lunches at the Algonquin Hotel.

Throughout the twenties, Parker wrote essays, short stories, and poems. In the late 1920s, she worked as a book reviewer for the *New Yorker* magazine. Her first poetry collection, *Enough Rope*, was published in 1926. Her story "Big Blonde" won the O. Henry Award as the year's best short story in 1929.

Parker became famous for her wry commentaries on modern life and culture and on male–female relations. She could be cruel, once remarking about a book: "This is not a novel to be tossed aside lightly. It should be thrown with great force."

Although many Americans were politically

DOROTHY PARKER built a career as a sharp-witted writer and reviewer.

sluggish in the 1920s and shied away from extreme views, Parker was committed to radical politics. In the late 1920s, she protested against the execution of anarchists Sacco and Vanzetti and attended Communist Party meetings.

In the early 1930s, Parker moved to Hollywood, where she worked as a screenwriter. In 1933 she helped found the Screen Writers Guild, a trade union for Hollywood writers. In the 1950s, anti-Communist fever swept the nation and Parker was blacklisted, meaning that Hollywood studios refused to hire her to write scripts. She returned to New York in 1963 and died in 1967.

Eugene O'Neill has been called the nation's greatest playwright. Like many other U.S. writers of the 1920s, his works were marked by experimentation and a rejection of traditional forms. O'Neill's plays most famously dug deep into the human psyche and often drew on characters and events from his own life and family.

O'Neill was born in New York City in 1888. His father, James O'Neill, was a professional actor, and Eugene spent part of his boyhood traveling from town to town where his father acted in plays. He eventually settled down to attend boarding schools in New York and Connecticut. O'Neill dropped out of Princeton University and began a vagabond life. He took jobs onboard ships and lived in port cities in the United States and overseas. After becoming sick with tuberculosis in 1912, O'Neill dedicated himself to writing plays.

For many years, O'Neill wrote short plays about his own experiences as a seaman. His first full-length play, *Beyond the Horizon*, opened on Broadway in 1920. Theater critics raved about *Beyond the Horizon*, and O'Neill earned his first of four Pulitzer Prizes for the effort. O'Neill was extremely prolific, with fifteen more plays produced just in the 1920s. The most famous of these were *The Emperor Jones*, *The Hairy Ape*, *Anna Christie*, *The Great God Brown*, and *Strange Interlude*. These plays broke with the realist tradition and used

EUGENE O'NEILL won Pulitzer Prizes for both drama and literature.

new approaches to staging. For instance, in *The Great Brown God*, characters wore masks to symbolize their hidden inner natures. In *Strange Interlude*, the actors gave spoken asides to the audience to express their inner thoughts. Several of O'Neill's plays from the decade examined themes from ancient Greek drama.

In the 1930s and 1940s, O'Neill's plays became more traditional and realistic, but they continued to explore the depths of the human soul. Several of these plays were directly based on O'Neill's own family struggles. Eugene O'Neill died in 1953. His acclaimed plays *Long Day's Journey into Night* and *A Moon for the Misbegotten* were not performed until after his death.

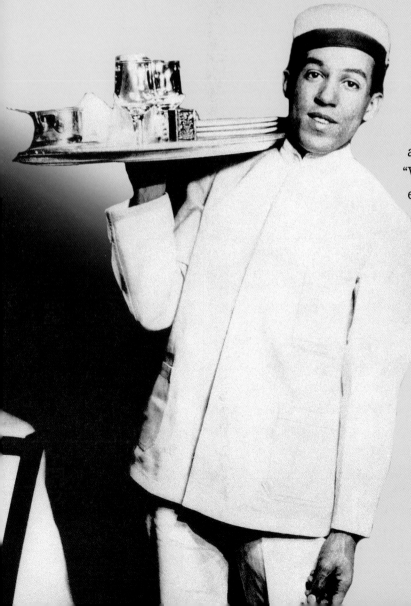

◼ HOME TO HARLEM

Uptown from the swank Round Table crowd at the Algonquin Hotel, the African American community of Harlem was a city unto itself. In was home to leading African artists and writers, as well as African American publications and national organizations. Many residents, recently arrived from the more racially repressive South, enjoyed a newfound sense of freedom, pride, and energy in Harlem. Throughout the 1920s, the neighborhood was the center of an extraordinary outburst of creative activity known as the Harlem Renaissance.

The Harlem Renaissance involved musicians, painters, and other artists. Writers were at the forefront, giving articulate voice to the African American experience. For instance, Langston Hughes spoke of African American pride, suffering, and longing in his acclaimed poem "Weary Blues" (1921) and later poems. In the novel *Home to Harlem*, Claude McKay explored the experiences of an African American soldier returning to the United States after World War I.

In 1925 **LANGSTON HUGHES** was working as a busboy at a hotel in Washington, D.C. He took the job to support himself while writing. By this time, "Weary Blues" and other poems had already been published in magazines and newspapers.

ZORA NEALE HURSTON arrived in New York City in 1925, at the peak of the Harlem Renaissance. She was there on a scholarship as the sole African American student at Manhattan's Barnard College.

Zora Neale Hurston wrote very precisely about her African American identity in her essay "How It Feels to Be Colored Me" (1928). Alaine Locke, a leader of the Harlem Renaissance, compiled essays, poetry, and stories written by dozens of African American writers into the collection *The New Negro* in 1925. The Harlem Renaissance continued beyond the 1920s, but the decade is considered its heyday—a time of great cultural awakening and the incubation period for the later civil rights movement.

■ READERS

Writers expressed themselves with great energy in the 1920s, but the other side of the equation was readers. To make a profit and to pay authors, publishers needed to get Americans excited about reading and get the latest books into their hands. Advertising executive Harry Scherman came up with a clever way to get the job done with the Book of the Month Club (BOMC), founded in 1926. The club mailed each paying member one new book per month, unless the member opted out on the book ahead of time. A five-member panel of well-known book critics screened the offerings, assuring members that only top-quality works reached their doorsteps. Americans loved the concept, and by 1929, BOMC had 111,000 members. Some BOMC selections, such as Sinclair Lewis's scathing *Elmer Gantry* (1927), a novel about religious fakery, are ranked as all-time classics. Many others, such as Edna Ferber's *Show Boat* (1926), were simply good, breezy reads.

The best-selling novel of the 1920s never rated high with literary critics, but ordinary Americans loved it. It was *The Man Nobody Knows* by advertising executive Bruce Barton. This inventive story combined two topics that Americans of the 1920s held dear: religion and business. The novel portrayed Jesus Christ as an ambitious and successful businessman—giving a boost to both Christian teaching and to probusiness philosophy in one neat literary package.

The 1920s witnessed the birth of several new magazines: *Reader's Digest* (1922) offered upbeat stories, practical advice, and patriotic messages. *Time* (1923) served up concise, thoughtful news analysis, and the *New Yorker* (1925) delved into literature, culture, and the arts. Each of these publications attracted legions of readers (and each remains in business in the twenty-first century). Americans also read newspapers regularly in the 1920s. Newspapers were the nation's primary news sources (with radio coming in second place). Most U.S. households subscribed to at least one daily paper.

" *The New Yorker* will be a reflection in word and picture of metropolitan life. It will be human. Its general tenor [tone] will be one of gaiety, wit and satire. . . . It will be what is commonly called sophisticated, in that it will assume a reasonable degree of enlightenment on the part of its readers."

—*New Yorker* statement, 1924

CHAPTER SEVEN

MODERN TIMES:
VISUAL ARTS OF THE 1920s

In 1920 artists Paul Strand and Charles Sheeler made a movie called *Manhatta*. The short film paid homage to Manhattan through a series of gritty moving images. The filmmakers focused their lens on soaring skyscrapers, belching smokestacks, busy construction sites, the intricate steel cables of the Brooklyn Bridge, and masses of people hustling down the streets of New York to their jobs. Strand was a photographer, and Sheeler was both a painter and a photographer. They made *Manhatta* as an artistic film—a commentary on the human-made environment, the stark and industrial scenes of urban life.

In the 1920s, industry, machinery, and commerce dramatically changed the American landscape. Strand, Sheeler, and other artists wanted to capture and record those changes. In 1927 Sheeler spent six weeks at the Ford Motor Company's River Rouge plant in Detroit, Michigan. There he photographed massive factory buildings, giant machines, and enormous crisscrossing conveyor belts. The resulting images were clean and hard edged. They portrayed industry as powerful and precise. Sheeler's pictures rarely showed the human element—the factory workers who tended the big machines or the dangerous nature of their work.

Like the photographers, painters of the 1920s also examined the commercial, industrialized world. *Lucky Strike* (1921) by Stuart Davis was a painting of a tobacco package.

Davis's *Odol* (1924) showed a bottle of mouthwash on a bathroom shelf. In addition to making photographs of industry, Charles Sheeler also painted railroad yards, factories, and other industrial scenes.

In 1922 Joseph Stella painted a view of the Brooklyn Bridge, which he described as a "metallic weird apparition under a steely sky . . . as the shrine containing all the efforts of the new civilization of AMERICA." Georgia O'Keeffe created *The Radiator Building—Night, New York*, in 1927. It shows a skyscraper with brightly lit windows, shining out into the surrounding darkness. In Stella's and O'Keeffe's paintings, the bridge and the building are much more than steel, stone, and concrete. They have magical energy. They seem alive and wide awake.

American painters and photographers of the 1920s were part of a larger art movement called modernism, which had its origins in Europe. Divided into categories such as cubism, constructivism, and futurism, modernist art cast aside soft lines and subtle shading in favor of more hard-edged and machinelike images—well suited to a decade of urbanism and industrialization.

Photographer and art promoter Alfred Stieglitz gathered around him a circle of American modernists in the 1920s. At a gallery show in New York, called Alfred Stieglitz Presents Seven Americans, he displayed the work of O'Keeffe (his wife), Strand, and himself, as well as that of Arthur Dove,

Italian American artist Joseph Stella completed this painting, *BROOKLYN BRIDGE*, in 1922. He painted the bridge many times during his career.

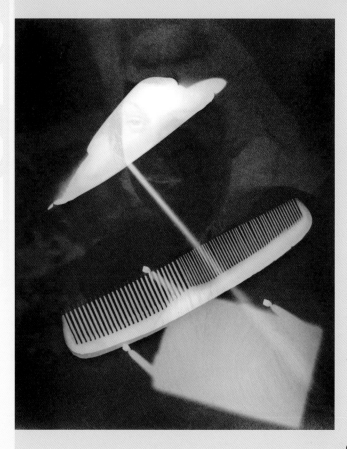

Man Ray used his cameraless photography method called **RAYOGRAPHY** to create this work, *Rayography comb*, in 1924.

Marsden Hartley, John Marin, and Charles Demuth. Later in the year, Stieglitz established a permanent gallery to show works by these same artists and others.

If Stieglitz and his contemporaries tested the boundaries of traditional art forms in the 1920s, Philadelphia-born Man Ray blew those boundaries to pieces. Ray (born Emmanuel Radnitzky) made art out of found materials, such as a household iron with metal tacks attached to the bottom. He embraced an art movement called Dada, whose practitioners created work that was deliberately absurd and irrational. Working from Paris after 1921, Ray also made surrealist films and photographs—with images that wove together strange, disconnected, and dreamlike elements. He developed a type of photograph called a rayograph, made without a camera and named for himself. His rayographs, made by placing objects on photographic paper and exposing them to light, showed images of simple household items such as thumbtacks and lightbulbs. Like Stuart Davis and others of the 1920s, Ray transformed everyday objects into more profound works of art.

■ DECO-RATION

In 1922 British archaeologist Howard Carter discovered the tomb of Tutankhamun, an ancient Egyptian pharaoh, better known as King Tut. The discovery was exciting, especially since Carter pulled all sorts of ancient Egyptian treasures from the tomb.

A lthough the Harlem Renaissance is most famous for its writers, a painter named Aaron Douglas was also at the core of this movement in the 1920s. Douglas was born in Topeka, Kansas, in 1898. He studied art at the University of Nebraska–Lincoln and graduated in 1922. After teaching art to schoolchildren for a few years, he moved to Harlem in 1925. He began making illustrations for the *Crisis* and *Opportunity*, the magazines of the NAACP and the National Urban League, respectively. Douglas refined his artistic style, incorporating elements of African and ancient Egyptian designs into his work. His use of hard edges, geometric patterns, and flattened forms gave his paintings a feeling reminiscent of African folk art.

Douglas's work illustrated *The New Negro* (1925), an anthology of writings by African Americans, and *God's Trombones* (1927), a book of poetry by Harlem Renaissance standout James Weldon Johnson. In 1934, working for the U.S. government's Works Progress Administration, Douglas created a series of murals for a branch of the New York Public Library. The murals

AARON DOUGLAS drew inspiration from African, American, and European art styles to create his paintings and murals.

depict scenes of African American life, including the great migration of African Americans to northern cities before and during World War I.

In 1937 Douglas joined the staff of Fisk University, an African American college in Nashville, Tennessee. He founded the university's art department and taught there for twenty-nine years. He died in 1979.

The **EGYPTIAN THEATRE** brought a little bit of ancient Egypt to Hollywood in the 1920s.

Back in the United States, the discovery kicked off a craze for all things ancient Egyptian. In Hollywood, theater owner Sid Grauman built the Egyptian Theatre, a 1,700-seat movie palace adorned with massive Egyptian-style columns, sphinx heads, dog-headed Egyptian gods, and hieroglyphics (Egyptian picture writing). Architects, furniture designers, fashion designers, and decorative artists all jumped on the ancient Egyptian bandwagon. Soon Americans were sporting everything from Cleopatra headdresses to cuff links decorated with hieroglyphics.

The Egyptian craze was just the beginning. For inspiration, designers of the 1920s also looked to the art of ancient America, Africa, and Asia. They incorporated trends from the visual arts, such as the jagged lines of cubism and constructivism. They drew inspiration from machine-age mass production. Finally, designers looked to the elegant styles coming out of Paris. The result was a captivating look called art deco. Hitting its stride after a 1925 decorative arts exposition in Paris, art deco combined sleek and streamline shapes, rich ornamentation, and sharp geometric patterns.

Art deco could be simple—a sleek, angular wristwatch, for instance. Art deco could also be ornate, as illustrated by the Eastern Columbia Building in Los Angeles. The building was covered in turquoise terra cotta and gold leaf and decorated inside and out with sunburst patterns, zigzags, and stylized plants and animals. With its soaring crown of terraced, stainless-steel arches

This elegant dining room in Louisville, Kentucky, features **ART DECO** furniture and wall treatments.

and tapering triangular windows, the seventy-seven-story Chrysler Building in Manhattan topped the list of 1920s art deco masterpieces. From advertising to ocean liners to movie sets, art deco was everywhere in the late 1920s. It was a style steeped in elegance, sophistication, and wealth.

> **" Ah, America . . . wonderful machinery, wonderful factories, wonderful buildings."**
>
> —*Louis Lozowick, "The Americanization of Art," essay for the Machine Age Exposition catalog, 1927*

■ THE LINE OF PARIS

Flapper fashion—particularly the short, sleeveless dress—is synonymous with the 1920s. In fact, the flapper look began in the mid-teens. Historians trace its origins to French fashion designer Coco Chanel. During the World War I years, while women in the United States were still wrapping themselves tightly in corsets, long sleeves, ruffles, and tight-waisted, ankle-length skirts, Chanel was moving into entirely new fashion territory. She made dresses that were sleeveless, silky, and simple. They fell straight at the waist and landed just below the knee.

The style caught on first in Paris and then among wealthy women in New York. By the early 1920s, Chanel's dress had become standard flapper attire in the United States. The "new silhouette" didn't suit every woman, however. It looked best on those with slim, boyish figures. The skinny, youthful set adored the flapper dress, while many older, heavier women clung to their long skirts and corsets.

It took more than a short dress to turn a female into a flapper. The young woman also needed to accessorize with a bell-shaped cloche hat, silk stockings, high-heeled shoes, beads, bangles, and a rhinestone handbag.

Makeup was also part of the ensemble. In earlier generations, only prostitutes and actresses had worn makeup. Painting one's face was a sign of loose morals, and "good girls" didn't do it. That rule had completely disappeared by the 1920s. Advertisers pushed women to buy face cream, lipstick, perfume, and hair dye, and women were quick to comply. The typical "Flapper Jane," as one news editor called her, was "heavily made up, not to imitate nature, but for an altogether artificial effect . . . poisonously scarlet lips, richly ringed eyes."

This model wears long strings of pearls with a **COCO CHANEL DRESS** of the late 1920s.

1920s PROFILE: John Held

The cover of *Life* magazine for the week of February 18, 1926, features a charming cartoon *(right)*. The center of attention is a fetching young flapper dancing the Charleston. Her dance partner is a distinguished, tuxedo-clad elderly gentleman, trying gamely to keep up with his young companion. The caption beneath the cartoon reads, "Teaching old dogs new tricks." The young woman dons standard flapper attire: a skimpy dress, silk stockings held up by garters, bangles on her arms, and a string of beads flying around her neck. She also sports a head of bobbed blonde hair. The cartoon was the work of John Held Jr. His whimsical pictures of flappers and their boyfriends helped spread the "flaming youth" stereotype far and wide in the 1920s.

Held was born in Salt Lake City, Utah, in 1889. As young as the age of three, he loved to draw pictures and make clay sculptures—a talent that he inherited from his father, a gifted artist and draftsman. After graduating from high school, Held became a cartoonist with the *Salt Lake Tribune.* His high school classmate Harold Ross worked there too, as a reporter.

In 1910 Held left Salt Lake City to work in New York City. He started out drawing advertising illustrations and soon was selling cartoons to *Judge*, *Puck*, *Vanity Fair*, *Life*, and other magazines. His clever pictures of "Betty Coed" (a flapper), "Joe College," and others won him an army of fans.

A flapper teaches new tricks to her dance partner on JOHN HELD'S 1926 *LIFE* MAGAZINE COVER.

By the 1920s, Harold Ross was also living in New York. Ross founded the *New Yorker* magazine in 1925, and Held's pictures often graced the magazine's covers.

John Held created a variety of artwork in the 1920s. He designed stage sets; illustrated book covers, including F. Scott Fitzgerald's *Flappers and Philosophers*; and produced a weekly comic strip called *Oh! Margy!* (Margy was a troublemaking flapper, naturally.) Held made a lot of money in the 1920s but lost most of it in the 1929 stock market crash. In the 1930s, he gave up cartooning in favor of painting and sculpture. He eventually retired to a farm in New Jersey, where he died in 1958.

This **FASHIONABLE FLAPPER** wears a tight-fitting cloche hat over her bobbed hair. Along with short hair and short skirts, many young women of the 1920s took up cigarettes.

Underneath the cloche hat, many flappers wore their hair cut short. When it debuted around 1915, the hair bob was yet another cause for alarm—a sign that young American women had lost their feminine virtues. By the early 1920s, however, the bobbed haircut was just one more fashion statement.

■ SMART SOCIETY

To keep pace with the flappers, men also had to look sharp. The typical college man of the 1920s slicked back his hair. He was clean shaven and went about his daily business in a cinched, belted jacket and "Oxford bags," which were wide-legged flannel trousers (first made fashionable by students at Oxford University in England).

Whether male or female, everyone dressed formally in the 1920s. Even gangsters wore three-piece suits when they rubbed out their gangland rivals. Out of doors, people always wore hats—even when sitting in the stands at a baseball game. Emily Post, whose *Etiquette in Society, in Business, and in Politics* appeared in 1922, offered this advice to gentlemen:

> The well-dressed man is always a paradox. He must look as though he gave his clothes no thought and as though literally they grew on him like a dog's fur, and yet he must be perfectly groomed. He must be close-shaved and have his hair cut and his nails in good order (not too polished). His linen must always be immaculate, his clothes "in press," his shoes perfectly "done." His brown shoes must shine like old mahogany, and his white buckskin must be whitened and polished like a prize bull terrier at a bench show. . . . The well-dressed man never wears the same suit or the same pair of shoes two days running.

Post was unapologetically a snob, and she offered her advice for the upper crust—those whose households included maids, butlers, and cooks. But in big U.S. cities, even the lower classes were surrounded by opulence—from glittering movie palaces to neon lights to store shelves overflowing with shiny new products. For fashion-conscious women on a budget, the latest "Modern Frocks in the New Silhouette—as New York Wears Them" were available by mail order from Sears, Roebuck for prices as low as $5.98.

Hollywood actor and producer Jack Coogan Sr. wears a **THREE-PIECE SUIT AND HAT.** Americans dressed formally in the 1920s, especially when going to work.

THE MUSEUM OF MODERN ART opened in a suite of rooms on the twelfth floor of the Heckscher Building in Manhattan in 1929.

In the past, Americans had looked to Europe for cues about art, fashion, and design. But World War I had all but devastated Europe, and the United States was quickly becoming an artistic beacon in its own right. When the Museum of Modern Art opened in New York in 1929, the nation took its place among the world's leading art centers. The cutting-edge, sleek, and industrialized United States was the place to be.

Showgirls from the ZIEGFELD FOLLIES pose with their performing dogs in the early 1920s.

CHAPTER EIGHT

SHOWTIME:
DRAMATIC ARTS OF THE 1920s

I f you wanted stardom in the early 1920s, the place to be was not Hollywood. The place to be was the Ziegfeld Follies in New York, the best show on Broadway. The Follies was a sumptuous live theatrical revue, replete with singing, dancing, and comedy. The highlight of the show was the sexy Ziegfeld Girls, who danced onstage in skimpy costumes. Comedian W. C. Fields, singer and comic Fanny Brice, cowboy humorist Will Rogers, and many other performers got their big breaks with Ziegfeld and went on to fame in movies and on radio.

Down the street from Ziegfeld, other musical shows pulled in crowds. *Lady, Be Good*, with music by brothers George and Ira Gershwin, opened at the Liberty Theatre on December 21, 1924. The show starred Adele Astaire and her brother Fred (who went on to sing and dance in movies) and featured the hit songs "Fascinating Rhythm" and "Oh, Lady Be Good." *No, No, Nanette*, which debuted on Broadway the following year, was most famous for launching the song "Tea for Two."

In 1927 *Show Boat* opened on Broadway. Based on a novel by Edna Ferber, the story was set on a nineteenth-century Mississippi River showboat, which provided a perfect setting for musical numbers penned by Jerome Kern and Oscar Hammerstein. The show later became a movie, and numbers such as "Ol' Man River" and "Can't Help Lovin'

Florenz Ziegfeld produced the Broadway hit **SHOW BOAT** in 1927. Many consider it to be the first Broadway musical.

Dat Man" took their place among the classics of American song.

Broadway's raunchier cousin was vaudeville, a label for variety shows held in small theaters all across the United States. Vaudeville shows featured a changing lineup of comics, acrobats, animal acts, jugglers, magicians, singers, dancers, and other performers. The talent wasn't always top notch, and some of the acts were crass. Nevertheless, vaudeville of the 1920s launched the careers of some big stars, including Jack Benny, George Burns, and the Marx Brothers—all comedians.

▇ THE SILVER SCREEN

The movies of the early 1920s were very different from modern-day films. For one thing, 1920s films were all black and white because color film had not yet been invented (although some films were tinted for special effect). Most important, the films of the early 1920s were silent. They had no spoken dialogue or other recorded sounds—again because the technology had not yet been developed. To provide dialogue and other information that viewers needed to understand the story, filmmakers inserted printed titles, or captions, in between scenes. As audiences watched the films in local theaters, live musicians played accompanying music to suit the mood of the action. The musicians ranged from a single piano player improvising along with the story line to whole orchestras playing music specifically composed for the film.

The king and queen of Hollywood in the early 1920s were Douglas Fairbanks Sr. and Mary Pickford—husband and wife and both stars of the silent screen. Along with comic actor Charlie Chaplin and film director D. W. Griffith, they had founded the United Artists movie studio in 1919.

In the 1926 film *THE BLACK PIRATE*, Douglas Fairbanks Sr. *(pushing on door)* plays a nobleman who becomes a pirate. In this guise, he rescues a young woman and takes revenge on the pirates who killed his father.

Fairbanks specialized in swashbucklers such as *The Mark of Zorro* (1920), *Robin Hood* (1922), and *The Black Pirate* (1926). Pickford—known as America's Sweetheart for her portrayal of wholesome, innocent young heroines—had played most of her starring roles in the 1910s and acted only occasionally in the 1920s.

In addition to United Artists, a host of other studios, including Paramount, Fox, MGM, RKO, and Warner Brothers, set up shop in Hollywood. Most films of this era were simple and cheap to make, and a single studio could easily churn out one per week. Across the United States, Americans hurried to hometown theaters to watch their favorite stars on the silver screen. In pictures such as *The Sheik* (1921) and *Blood and Sand* (1922), dark and handsome Rudolph Valentino made female moviegoers swoon. (When he died unexpectedly in 1926, distraught fans caused a near riot at his funeral.) Swedish import Greta Garbo, brooding and mysterious, was another fan favorite.

> **"When I saw Rudolph Valentino in 'The Sheik,' I could do nothing but think of him for days to follow. Several of my girl friends and I sent to Hollywood for the star's picture."**
>
> —*Female moviegoer, 1921*

■ YOUNG FELLOWS

Charlie Chaplin was already a superstar when the 1920s began. In film after film in the 1910s, he had played a character called the Tramp. Dressed in shabby, ill-fitting clothing, the Tramp was hapless and penniless—constantly getting knocked around by life but always rebounding in the end. Chaplin, a native of London, England, and a shrewd businessman in real life, acted in only a few films in the 1920s, most notably *The Kid* (1921) and *The Gold Rush* (1925), in which he reprised his Tramp character.

Picking up the mantle from Chaplin, Harold Lloyd also created an endearing silent film persona—a bespectacled young man who comes to the big city seeking fortune and quickly finds himself overwhelmed. In the classic *Safety Last* (1923), Lloyd must scale a tall city building, a harrowing feat that left movie audiences on the edge of their seats. The final thrilling scene, in which Lloyd dangles from the hands of a giant clock on the side of the building, has gone down as one of the greatest in movie history.

Like Chaplin and Lloyd, Buster Keaton always portrayed a determined young man who finds ways to triumph over adversity. In *The General* (1927), Keaton plays a railroad engineer named Johnny Gray. Unable to enlist in the Confederate (Southern) army during the Civil War (1861–1865), Johnny nevertheless manages to foil the Union (Northern) forces. He ends the film as a hero—and also gets the girl.

Harold Lloyd dangles perilously in the closing scene of the 1923 silent film *SAFETY LAST*.

Actress Clara Bow plays flapper Betty Lou Spence in **1927'S HIT FILM** *IT*.

■ IT

In 1926 a British novelist named Elinor Glyn wrote a juicy story called *It*. The protagonist was a fun-loving flapper named Betty Lou Spence. According to Glyn, Betty Lou had a certain "animal magnetism"—"the 'open sesame' to success in life and love." This special something was a quality that some called sex appeal and Glyn called It.

The next year, *It* became a Hollywood film starring Clara Bow. Dubbed the It Girl, Bow indeed had sex appeal. She displayed it in dozens of 1920s films with titles such as *The Adventurous Sex, My Lady's Lips, Kiss Me Again, Dance Madness, The Wild Party,* and *Dangerous Curves.*

Bow was not alone in putting the flapper on the big screen. Louise Brooks played flapper roles in films such as *Love 'Em and Leave 'Em, Rolled Stockings, The City Gone Wild,* and her most famous *Pandora's Box.* Colleen Moore shot to stardom in *Flaming Youth* in 1923. With that film, her flapper persona was sealed. She went on to act in *The Perfect Flapper, Flirting with Love, Why Be Good?* and similar Jazz Age silents. These movies all featured generous doses of flirting, drinking, dancing, and partygoing.

The public ate up the pictures and read about the stars' hobbies, pets, and favorite foods in movie magazines such as *Photoplay.* What the fan magazines didn't say was that Hollywood flappers and their beaus often carried on much like their on-screen personas—sometimes far more outrageously. In the early 1920s, several Hollywood actors and directors were caught up in scandals involving murder, rape, and drug taking. "Hollywood is a colony of . . . people where debauchery [moral corruption], riotous living, drunkenness . . . [and] free love seem to be conspicuous," roared one U.S. senator, insisting that the movie industry clean up its act.

101

Mae West was a sex symbol of the 1920s, but she was not the skinny flapper or It Girl type. West was busty and curvaceous. She wore tight-fitting, ornate gowns, big hats, furs, and jewels. An actor and playwright, she caused a scandal on Broadway with her bawdy stage shows.

Mary Jane West, nicknamed Mae, was born in Brooklyn, New York, in 1892. At the age of seven, she began singing and dancing in talent shows. She joined the professional vaudeville circuit at the age of fourteen and soon worked her way into Broadway revues.

In the 1920s West started writing her own plays, using the pen name Jane Mast. West's play *Sex* (1926), which she wrote, produced, directed, and starred in, followed the adventures of a saucy prostitute named Margy Lamont. The authorities thought that *Sex* had far too much sex. They had West arrested for indecency, for which she spent eight days in jail as punishment. Her next play, *The Drag*, dealt openly with homosexuality, a taboo topic at the time. That play was banned from Broadway. West's other plays of this era included *The Wicked Age, Pleasure Man, The Constant Sinner,* and her hit *Diamond Lil*.

In 1932 West moved to Hollywood, where she wrote screenplays for and act-

MAE WEST played sexy, witty women—much like herself—onstage and in the movies.

ed in several movies, always playing the bawdy, wisecracking blonde. The movie censors were constantly trying to rid her scripts of sexy scenes and dirty jokes, with only partial success. From the 1940s through the 1970s, West performed only occasionally in movies, onstage, and on television. After suffering a stroke, she died in 1980.

WILLIAM H. HAYS resigned his position as U.S. postmaster general to become the first president of the Motion Picture Producers and Distributors of America in 1922.

In 1922 the studio heads agreed to rein in the actors. Banding together as the Motion Picture Producers and Distributors of America (MPPDA), the studios insisted that stars sign "morals clauses" in their contracts—agreeing to good offscreen behavior if they wanted to keep their jobs. At first the MPPDA didn't censor movies themselves, but as films got racier throughout the decade, there were increased cries for censorship. Finally, in 1930, religious leaders and others pushed the MPPDA to adopt a code of restrictions, with a long list of themes, scenes, and language that were off-limits to moviemakers. (The code wasn't strictly enforced until 1934.)

■ "YOU AIN'T HEARD NOTHIN' YET"

In the early 1920s, engineers worked feverishly to figure out how to make movies with sound. In 1925 the Bell Telephone Company finally developed a successful sound system called Vitaphone. Warner Brothers was the first movie studio to give the system a try. In 1926 Warner made *Don Juan*, a swashbuckler with a Vitaphone sound track. The movie didn't have any spoken dialogue, but it did have a lush musical background played by the New York Philharmonic Orchestra. It also included sound effects such as the clashing and clanging of swords.

The following year, Warner Brothers premiered the first real "talkie"—a movie with spoken dialogue—*The Jazz Singer* starring Al Jolson. *The Jazz Singer* didn't embrace sound entirely. Most of the dialogue was still printed on title cards. But the sound track included both singing and orchestra music. And about twenty minutes into the movie, Jolson uttered the first words ever spoken on film: "Wait a minute, wait a minute, you ain't heard nothin' yet."

Al Jolson performs the final scene in the first talking film, *THE JAZZ SINGER*, in 1927. Jolson plays a Jewish man who becomes a popular singer. In this scene, he wears blackface makeup, a theatrical style that emphasizes racist stereotypes of African Americans.

The film was a sensation, and in the next few years, all the major studios transitioned to talking pictures. Some of the silent stars panicked. The studios made them take voice tests, and a lot of them didn't make the cut. For instance, the exotic Polish-born Pola Negri had been a favorite in silent films. But when Negri spoke in the talkies, audiences didn't like her thick Polish accent. So Negri left Hollywood and made movies in Europe. Greta Garbo had a Swedish accent, but audiences loved it, and she remained a star through the 1930s.

By the late 1920s, the movies had become a vital part of American cultural life. The movie studios were prosperous businesses employing thousands. Hollywood took the opportunity to pat itself on the back in 1929 with the first ever Academy Awards. At a ceremony in Hollywood, the Academy of Motion Picture Arts and Sciences handed out twelve awards for achievement in acting and moviemaking. The top award, for Outstanding Picture, went to *Wings*, a movie about World War I flyers (starring Clara Bow, among others).

In the movies of the 1920s, black actors were rarely seen. When they did appear, they played simple-minded servants or slaves, menacing villains, or ferocious natives in the African jungle. In some Hollywood films, such as *The Jazz Singer*, white actors appeared in black-face—with their skin darkened into cartoonish masks.

African American moviegoers who wanted to see blacks depicted respectfully on the screen had one option. Specially made "race movies" featured all-black casts and showed at theaters in black neighborhoods.

In the 1920s, the leading producer of race movies was Oscar Micheaux. Born in 1884, the son of former slaves, Micheaux grew up in Great Bend, Kansas. In an age when African Americans were restricted to certain jobs and neighborhoods, Micheaux did something unusual. For several years, he farmed a piece of land in South Dakota—a state that was nearly all white. He also began writing fiction.

As the movies grew in popularity, Micheaux founded his own movie studio, the Micheaux Film and Book Company in Chicago. His first film, *The Homesteader* (1919), was based on his own novel, which itself was based on his experiences farming in South Dakota. *The Homesteader* was the first feature-length film made by an African American.

OSCAR MICHEAUX made race movies, which had all-black casts and showed at theaters in African American neighborhoods.

Micheaux made more than thirty films in the 1920s, 1930s, and 1940s, including dramas, romances, and comedies. The films explored themes such as racial injustice and marriage between blacks and whites. The characters were always portrayed with dignity. Several black actors who later crossed over into mainstream Hollywood films, most notably Paul Robeson, got their start acting for Oscar Micheaux.

Performers from a traveling musical revue dance at CHICAGO'S SUNSET CLUB around 1922. Housed in a former automobile garage, the Sunset Club became one of Chicago's legendary jazz venues.

CHAPTER NINE

THE JAZZ AGE:
MUSIC OF THE 1920s

Music was everywhere in the 1920s—in speakeasies, in Broadway and vaudeville shows, on the radio, and on records. Composers such as Irving Berlin, Cole Porter, and George Gershwin penned catchy melodies and lyrics for musical shows. Jazz players such as Duke Ellington and Louis Armstrong put on dazzling live performances. "There was so much music in the air that if you held up a horn, it would play by itself," joked one Chicago jazz musician.

Americans also played music at home and in schools on pianos, accordions, ukuleles, and other instruments. After hearing a song on the radio, people often rushed out to buy the sheet music or the record. Songs such as "Yes! We Have No Bananas" and "Ain't We Got Fun" captured the playfulness of the decade.

■ BLACK AND TAN

Jazz music swept through the United States like a storm in the 1920s. Jazz had traveled north from New Orleans with the great migration of African Americans in the 1910s. Chicago, Kansas City, and New York became hot spots for African American jazz musicians and jazz clubs.

Early in the 1920s, white musicians grabbed onto jazz, learning and borrowing from the black jazz players. Despite this sharing, jazz bands of this era were segregated.

Composer George Gershwin embraced a unique musical mix in the 1920s. With his lyricist brother Ira, he wrote catchy show tunes such as "I Got Rhythm." But on his own, Gershwin crafted elaborate orchestral pieces, including the famed *Rhapsody in Blue.*

Gershwin was born in Brooklyn, New York, in 1898. At the age of thirteen, he began studying classical piano, but he also had a knack for writing show tunes. At the age of fifteen, George quit school to work as a songwriter on Tin Pan Alley—the center of the music publishing business in Manhattan. In 1919 he wrote the popular song "Swanee" for a New York revue. Singer Al Jolson put the song on record in 1920, and it became a runaway best seller, with sky-high record and sheet music sales.

George's older brother Ira, meanwhile, discovered his talent for penning clever poetry and verse. He wrote lyrics for Broadway shows, and in 1924, the brothers teamed up to write *Lady, Be Good*. But George had not abandoned his interest in concert music. Also in 1924, he composed *Rhapsody in Blue*. This long work for piano and jazz band combined elements of classical music and jazz—a combination never explored before. Critics hailed it as a modern American masterwork.

Back on Tin Pan Alley, George and Ira continued to write Broadway shows. Then George once again veered toward the classical side with *An American in Paris* (1928).

GEORGE GERSHWIN created popular songs as well as classical masterpieces in the 1920s.

This poetic piece again broke new musical ground—combining the classical sounds of a symphonic orchestra with saxophone and even car horns.

The brothers' last great collaboration was *Porgy and Bess* (1935), which George called a folk opera. The story explores the daily struggles of residents of Catfish Row, a poor African American neighborhood in Charleston, South Carolina. In composing the music, George drew inspiration from traditional African American music such as blues and gospel singing.

Only thirty-eight years old, George Gershwin died of a brain tumor in 1937. Teaming up with other musicians, Ira continued to write lyrics for Broadway shows and Hollywood movies. He died in 1983.

DUKE ELLINGTON *(RIGHT)* **AND HIS OR-CHESTRA** performed at the Cotton Club in New York and on the radio.

Black bandleaders such as Fletcher Henderson, King Oliver, and Duke Ellington headed all-black bands. Whites such as Bix Beiderbecke and Paul Whiteman led all-white bands. Nightly, urbane white New Yorkers congregated at the Cotton Club, a white-owned speakeasy in Harlem, to hear Duke Ellington's band. But except for the performers, blacks were not welcome in the Cotton Club and other popular speakeasies. Only a few "black and tan" clubs welcomed patrons of both races.

The larger music industry was also segregated. Mainstream, white-owned music companies, such as Okeh Records in New York, focused mainly on recording the work of white performers and selling records to a white audience. But Okeh also produced "race records"—recordings by black bands and singers marketed specifically to African Americans. Throughout most of the 1920s, national radio shows wouldn't play the music of black artists. But in 1927, the CBS radio corporation brought a microphone into the Cotton Club and finally broadcast a black jazz band—Duke Ellington's orchestra—to a national audience.

> **"What a mob, what a mob. Never have seen the club so jammed. Not a spot the size of a dime on the floor. And why I ask you. Because there is only one band like this every thousand years."**
>
> —*master of ceremonies introducing Duke Ellington and band at the Cotton Club, 1929*

Some whites thought that jazz music—with its blaring horns and unconventional rhythms—was sinful. Because it originated with African Americans, they called it "jungle music"—a derogatory reference to the jungles of Africa. Some Americans charged that jazz stirred up the basest, most vulgar human instincts and contributed to the corruption of young people. "Moral disaster is coming to hundreds of American girls through the pathological [unhealthy] nerve-exciting music of jazz orchestras," wrote the *New York American* in 1922. "According to the Illinois Vigilance Association, in Chicago alone the association's representatives have traced the fall of one thousand girls in the last two years to jazz music."

■ WAY DOWN SOUTH

Like jazz, the blues had their origins in southern black culture, specifically in the work songs, spirituals, and ballads of African American slaves. Like jazz, blues migrated from South to North with African Americans in the early twentieth century. Unlike jazz, the blues never really caught on with the white mainstream in the 1920s. Blues singers performed mostly at black clubs for black audiences and recorded their work on race records. The most acclaimed blues singer of the 1920s was Bessie Smith, beloved for her soulful performances and nicknamed the Queen of the Blues. The world of blues and jazz overlapped quite a bit in the 1920s. For instance, Bessie Smith made a number of recordings with jazz trumpeter Louis Armstrong. For the most part, however, blues stayed firmly in the black community, while jazz jumped across racial barriers.

BLUES SINGER BESSIE SMITH got her start performing with her brother on the streets of her hometown of Chattanooga, Tennessee.

The name Louis Armstrong is inseparable from 1920s jazz. A native of New Orleans, Armstrong grew up steeped in the city's rich jazz heritage. As a boy, he listened to King Oliver's Creole Jazz Band and other top groups. He taught himself to play cornet at the age of eleven. Extremely poor, Armstrong was in and out of trouble as a youth, but he continued to play cornet as well as trumpet. He soon earned a living playing in dance halls and on the steamboats that cruised up and down the Mississippi River.

In 1922 Armstrong joined a steady stream of African Americans moving north to Chicago, where jobs were plentiful. King Oliver had come to Chicago several years before, and Armstrong joined his Creole Jazz Band there. Two years later, Armstrong moved to New York to play trumpet with the Fletcher Henderson Orchestra at the high-end Roseland Ballroom (which welcomed only white patrons). By then Armstrong had sealed his reputation as one of the most skillful horn players in the nation. He created brilliant improvisational solos. He was also a talented singer.

Armstrong returned to Chicago in 1925. He began to perform and make records with his own band, Louis Armstrong and the Hot Five (sometimes the Hot Seven). His recording of King Oliver's "West End Blues" from this era is considered a jazz masterpiece. Armstrong added to his repertoire by

LOUIS ARMSTRONG brought jazz music to venues across the United States and all around the world.

scat singing, or improvising with nonsense syllables. Returning to New York in 1929 he performed with the show *Hot Chocolate* an all-black revue. His rendition of Fats Waller's "Ain't Misbehavin'" from this show won rave reviews.

By 1930 Louis Armstrong was a full-fledged jazz superstar. For the next several decades, he led his own band the All-Stars made recordings, and performed in movies and live shows, on radio, and on television. As he grew older, he focused more on singing than on horn playing. Armstrong died of a heart attack in 1971. He is remembered as the greatest jazz artist of the twentieth century.

A country music radio show called ***NATIONAL BARN DANCE*** offered skits and music to studio audiences and radio listeners. This performer played a character called the High Esteemed Cider Sipper.

As they did with "race music," Okeh and other record companies tried to pigeonhole country music in the 1920s. They called it hillbilly music and marketed it to poor white southerners. But music is hard to pigeonhole. For instance, country music of the 1920s had a lot in common with the blues. Many of the songs and rhythms were the same. But this was an era of segregation, especially in the South, and country music developed as a distinctly white genre. Accompanying themselves on guitars, banjos, and fiddles, performers such as the Carter Family and the Skillet Lickers sang old folk songs, ballads, and hymns. They made records and performed at musical shows and dances. The first country radio show was the *National Barn Dance*, broadcast out of Nashville, Tennessee, in 1924. The name changed to the *Grand Ole Opry* in 1928.

■ RUNNIN' WILD

Dance was an integral part of 1920s social life. All towns had dance bands that performed nightly, and big cities had large dance orchestras. At ballrooms, schools, and community centers, couples danced the waltz and the fox-trot, and even the sexy tango. But then jazz music boomed, and dances became more athletic.

The Charleston, named after a song of the same name, debuted in the Broadway show *Runnin' Wild* in 1923. The Charleston was the most typical flapper dance. Images of the era, such as John Held's cartoons, often show skinny, long-limbed flappers kicking their legs and swinging their arms mid-dance.

Rivaling the Charleston in popularity was the Black Bottom, a dance with its origins in the rural African American South. Dancers showed off the Black Bottom in the stage show *Dinah* in 1924 and two years later in George White's Scandals, a popular Broadway revue. Soon, partygoers were all cutting loose with the Black Bottom, which involved stomping the feet, gyrating at the hips, and swaying the arms.

Flappers dance in a **CHARLESTON CONTEST** at New York City's Parody Club in 1926.

In 1927 three hundred couples competed in a **MARATHON DANCE,** which involved dancing the 15 miles (24 km) from Venice to Los Angeles, California. The winning couple earned a cash prize.

Dance marathons were a 1920s craze in which couples danced for as long as they could. Eventually, contestants quit or gave up in exhaustion, and the last couple standing won a cash prize. A couple in Cleveland set the record in 1923 by dancing for ninety hours and ten minutes—almost four days straight.

Professional dancers covered all the angles in the 1920s. Touring the United States with their Denishawn Dance Company, Los Angeles–based Ruth St. Denis and Ted Shawn introduced Americans to the unfamiliar world of modern dance. This kind of dance—a rejection of the scripted movements of ballet—featured spontaneous and free-flowing movement, with dancers using their bodies to express a range of feelings.

JOSEPHINE BAKER shows off an elaborate, feathered costume at a show in 1926.

More familiar to American audiences, the Ziegfeld Girls of the Ziegfeld Follies danced in a chorus line with big feathered headdresses and skimpy costumes. The dancers at the Cotton Club—a troupe of light-skinned African American women, also scantily clad—were billed as "tall, tan, and terrific." Showing the most skin of all was Josephine Baker, originally from Saint Louis, Missouri. She began dancing at black clubs and musical shows in New York City and then moved to Paris, where she became a star at the Folies Bergère in the mid-1920s. Dancing in outrageous costumes (including a skirt made out of a string of fake bananas) and sometimes nearly naked, she wowed French audiences. Although she did not rise to the same level of stardom in the United States, she greatly influenced future generations of African American performers.

Baseball sensation BABE RUTH swings at a pitch during a game in the early 1920s.

CHAPTER TEN

PLAY BALL:
SPORTS AND GAMES

Big-league baseball needed a morale booster in 1920. The previous year had seen the notorious Black Sox Scandal, in which eight Chicago White Sox players were accused of deliberately losing the World Series to the Cincinnati Reds in exchange for payments from gamblers. Fans were disgusted that ballplayers would behave so shamefully. They needed a new hero, and they found one in George Herman "Babe" Ruth. In 1920, when he signed with the New York Yankees for a staggering $125,000, he launched baseball into its golden age.

When Ruth came to New York from the Boston Red Sox, the Yankees had never won a pennant. But during the next eight years, he led his teammates to six pennants and two World Series victories. The triple-decked Yankee Stadium, which opened in 1923, had seats for sixty thousand fans and the first ever electric scoreboard. Commentators called the stadium the House That Ruth Built because he created so much excitement and income for Yankees baseball.

Ruth's greatest single season was 1927, when he slammed sixty home runs, setting a record that stood for more than thirty years. For the rest of the 1920s and into the 1930s, Babe Ruth ruled as the baseball's home-run king. His records of 714 career home runs stood until 1974.

THE CHICAGO AMERICAN GIANTS captured their third Negro National League title in 1922, the year this photo was taken.

Baseball fans of the 1920s filled the seats at big-city stadiums and also listened to games on radio. The players gave them much to cheer about. The same year Ruth hit sixty home runs, his Yankee teammate Lou Gehrig knocked forty-seven home runs into the bleachers. George Sisler of the Saint Louis Browns had a remarkable batting average of .420 in 1922, while Rogers Hornsby, who played for three different National League teams in the 1920s, hit over .400 in three years. Great pitchers of the era included Grover Cleveland Alexander, Carl Mays, and Lefty Grove.

The big leagues of the 1920s allowed no African American players, however. Baseball was strictly segregated, and blacks played in separate "Negro Leagues"—the Eastern Colored League and the Negro National League. Black players such as James "Cool Papa" Bell, Leroy "Satchel" Paige, and Judy Johnson were almost unknown in this era—but not for a lack of talent. White fans and the media largely ignored the Negro Leagues and their stars. It wasn't until the late twentieth century, after many of the players had died, that the Negro League players finally got recognition.

■ GRIDIRON

In football in the 1920s, most of the excitement was in the college ranks, and the most famous college player was Harold "Red" Grange of the University of Illinois. Grange was a good punter, passer, and blocker, but as a broken-field runner, he was sensational. He was extremely fast. He twisted and turned as he crisscrossed the field, shedding tacklers in his wake. The press nicknamed him the Galloping Ghost because he was so hard to hang on to.

The Galloping Ghost had many brilliant afternoons on the gridiron, but perhaps his greatest single performance was against the University of Michigan in 1924. On the opening kickoff, Grange caught the ball on his own 5-yard line and ran 95 yards for a touchdown. He ran 67, 55, and 45 yards for three more touchdowns before the game was twelve minutes old.

Undoubtedly the greatest football coach of the decade was Knute Rockne. He played for the University of Notre Dame "Fighting Irish" from 1911 to 1913 and coached the school's team from 1918 to 1931 (when he died in an airplane crash). During this time, his teams tallied a record of 105 wins, twelve losses, and five ties.

Rockne couldn't have achieved his remarkable success without a talented squad of players. His backfield from 1922 to 1924 consisted of quarterback Harry Stuhldreher, right halfback Don Miller, left halfback Jim Crowley, and fullback Elmer Layden, nicknamed the Four Horsemen of Notre Dame. As a unit, the Four Horseman played thirty games and lost only two.

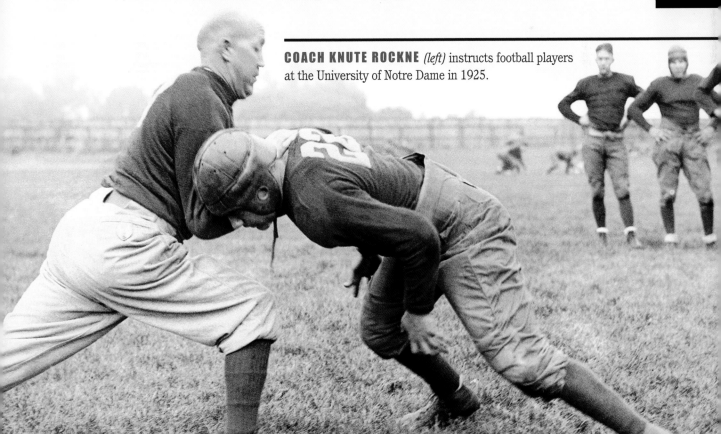

COACH KNUTE ROCKNE *(left)* instructs football players at the University of Notre Dame in 1925.

HAROLD "RED" GRANGE signed with the Chicago Bears in 1925, the day after he graduated from college. This photo comes from a December 1925 game.

As fans were cheering their college favorites, professional football was just getting organized. The American Professional Football Association was formed in 1920 and renamed the National Football League in 1922. At first, professional teams attracted little attention. But in 1925, Red Grange joined the Chicago Bears, and fans took notice. Attendance at professional games increased steadily through the decade. The end of the decade saw the rise of the Green Bay Packers, who won three consecutive championships from 1929 to 1931.

■ GOOD SPORTS

Competitive swimming didn't have many fans in the early twentieth century—until Johnny Weissmuller hit the pool. Weissmuller was born in Germany, and he immigrated to the United States with his family when he was an infant. In 1921, only sixteen, he won national swimming titles at 50 and 220 yards (46 and 202 m). By 1928 Weissmuller held every freestyle world record, from 100 yards (91 m) to a half mile (0.8 km), and possessed five Olympic gold medals. At 6 feet 3 inches (190 centimeters) tall, broad-chested, muscular, and handsome, Weissmuller looked good on camera. So he retired from competition in 1929 and turned his athletic talents into an acting career. In the 1930s and 1940s, he made a living portraying Tarzan in Hollywood movies.

Like swimming, tennis did not attract legions of fans, but it nevertheless produced champions in the 1920s. Bill Tilden, a Californian, had a fierce serve and all-round court brilliance. From 1920 to 1929, he was the number-one-ranked player in the United States. During that time, he won the American National Title seven times, Britain's Wimbledon championships three times, and seventeen of twenty U.S. Davis Cup singles matches. Helen Wills, also of California, was the nation's premier female tennis player. She was national women's champion seven times between 1923 and 1931 and won at Wimbledon eight straight times, beginning in 1927.

Golf was for amateurs only until U.S. golfers created the Professional Golfers Association in 1916. Shortly afterward, golf had its first superstars. One of them was Bobby Jones of Atlanta, Georgia. Between 1923 and 1930, Jones won thirteen major championships, including the U.S. Open, the British Open, and the U.S. Amateur. In 1930 he made a grand slam by winning the British Open, the British Amateur, the U.S. Open, and the U.S. Amateur in one year. Afterward, millions of admirers cheered him at a ticker-tape parade in New York City, followed by a reception at city hall with Mayor Jimmy Walker.

HELEN WILLS dives for the return during the 1927 Wimbledon tennis tournament. She emerged the champion that year.

Endurance swimmer GERTRUDE EDERLE cuts through cold waters in her 1926 swim across the English Channel.

Gertrude Ederle shared the swimming spotlight with Johnny Weissmuller in 1926 when she became the first woman to swim across the English Channel—the body of water that separates Great Britain from France. Only five men had previously accomplished this feat, and Ederle swam faster than all of them.

Ederle was born in 1906 in New York City. She learned to swim at her family's riverside cottage in New Jersey. As a teenager, she trained with the Women's Swimming Association in New York. In 1922, at the age of fifteen, she entered a 3.5-mile (5.6 km) race for women across New York Bay. She stunned the swimming world by beating fifty-one other competitors in the race, including U.S. and British champions. In the following few years, Ederle picked up dozens of swimming titles and knocked down nine world records. She won a gold and two bronze medals at the 1924 Olympics in Paris.

In August 1925, after covering her body with grease to protect her from the cold, Ederle made her first attempt to swim the English Channel from France to Great Britain.

After nine hours in the choppy water, she got seasick, and her trainer insisted that she quit. Ederle fired that trainer, hired a new one, and resolved to try again the next summer.

In August 1926, Ederle again set out across the English Channel from the French side. The seas quickly turned ugly. Ederle crawled on against high winds and waves. Her support staff, following in a boat, urged her to quit, but she refused. When she reached the British town of Kingsdown, fourteen hours and thirty-nine minutes later, she was hailed as a hero. She had swum 35 miles (56 km) and beat the previous English Channel-crossing record by almost two hours.

Back in the United States, Ederle tried to turn her swimming prowess into a show business career. She played herself in a 1927 movie and performed in water shows. But that work sputtered out. Gradually, Ederle lost her hearing—an affliction stemming from a case of childhood measles and prolonged exposure to cold water during endurance swims. For many years after she went deaf, Ederle taught swimming to deaf children. She died in 2003.

Rivaling Jones in the limelight was Walter Hagen, who won eleven major tournaments between 1914 and 1929. His skill on the golf course, combined with his flashy clothing and larger-than-life personality, helped attract many spectators to the sport in the 1920s. Hagen was the first player to earn more than one million dollars playing golf.

One of the biggest names in sports in the 1920s was not a person but a horse—the racehorse Man o' War. His career lasted just two years (1919 and 1920), but in those years, he earned a permanent place in horse-racing history. In his very first race in 1919, he won by six lengths. From then on, he was the favorite in every race he ran. In his short career, he won twenty out of twenty-one races, setting a slew of track and world records and winning the prestigious Preakness and Belmont Stakes. His only loss, in 1919, was to the aptly named Upset.

At the 1920 Dwyer Stakes race at the Aqueduct track in New York, **MAN O' WAR** *(right)* set a new U.S. record of one minute and forty-nine seconds on a course of just over 1 mile (1.6 km).

Boxing enjoyed enormous popularity in the 1920s, and for much of the decade, Jack Dempsey was king of the ring. Dempsey was born in Colorado in 1895. His family was poor, and he began boxing to earn money. Throughout the 1910s, he honed his skills, taking fights where he could find them.

Dempsey hit the big time in 1918, when he bowled over a row of heavyweights with one-round knockouts. Ring fans had never seen anything like his savage, two-handed attack. He was all fighter—with whipcord muscles and weighing a lean 190 pounds (86 kilograms).

On July 4, 1919, he fought champion Jess Willard for the heavyweight title. Willard was a huge man, but Dempsey blasted him to the canvas seven times in the first round. By the end of the third round, Willard had surrendered.

Dempsey successfully defended his title against Georges Carpentier in 1921 and Luis Firpo in 1923. In 1926 Dempsey took on soft-spoken challenger Gene Tunney. Few people thought Tunney had any chance of winning, but they were proven wrong. In the fight on September 24, 1926, before 120,000 fans, Tunney outboxed Dempsey and took the heavyweight title.

A Tunney–Dempsey rematch was arranged for September 22, 1927. For six rounds, Tunney outboxed his opponent. In the seventh round, Dempsey caught Tunney

CHAMPION BOXER JACK DEMPSEY throws a punch during training in Michigan City, Indiana, around 1922.

in a corner and knocked him to the ground. In what is called the long count, Dempsey refused to go to his corner after Tunney fell, so the referee delayed starting the normal ten-second count.

The delay gave Tunney a few extra seconds to recover. He got up at the count of nine, and Dempsey flew toward him. But Tunney backpedaled and circled out of range until his head cleared. He recovered completely in the next round and won the bout.

After losing his title, Dempsey retired from professional boxing. He boxed in exhibition matches and served in the National Guard and Coast Guard during World War II (1939–1945). He later wrote several books about boxing and his career. He died in 1977.

■ AMUSEMENTS

Americans of the 1920s were avid sports fans, and they enthusiastically followed the exploits of Babe Ruth, Red Grange, and others on radio and in the newspaper. But the typical American of the 1920s wasn't all that athletic. For many people, the occasional game of bowling or a Saturday night dance was their only workout.

Americans were definitely joiners in the 1920s. Businessmen joined the Rotary, Elks, Kiwanis, and similar clubs, which were focused on business networking, community service, and socializing. Women who did not hold paying jobs often worked unpaid for charity organizations, church clubs, and civic associations. The Boy Scouts and Girl Scouts were popular among young people. Teens also joined school bands, academic clubs, and sports teams.

Playing cards, especially bridge, was a very popular 1920s pastime. Reading was always a favorite. Crossword puzzles were wildly popular, especially after publisher Simon and Schuster released its first *Crossword Puzzle Book* in 1924.

GIRL SCOUTS practice with signal flags around 1920.

WOMEN PLAY MAH-JONGG on a floating game board at a pool in 1924.

In addition to these fairly ordinary activities, Americans of the 1920s also spent time in some unexpected and unusual ways. Fads swept the country, starting with the mah-jongg craze. Mah-jongg is a Chinese game, similar to the card game rummy but played with rectangular tiles engraved with Chinese drawings and symbols. In a passion for all things Chinese, Americans embraced the game in the early 1920s, buying as many as 1.6 million mah-jongg sets in just a few years.

After mah-jongg, the marathon dance craze took over, with sleepless couples dragging themselves wearily across the dance floor in a quest for cash prizes. Next came flagpole sitting. This craze began in 1924 when Hollywood stuntman Alvin "Shipwreck" Kelly, responding to a dare, parked himself on a platform atop a flagpole on a Los Angeles hotel. Kelly sat for thirteen hours and thirteen minutes, and a new craze took off. Across the United States, people erected flagpoles and perched for hours on end while crowds eyed them from below. To keep the crowds coming, local businesses often sponsored the exhibitions. Despite efforts to surpass him, Alvin Kelly remained king of the pole, repeating his feat across the nation and finally staying aloft for a record forty-nine days in Atlantic City in 1930.

ALVIN "SHIPWRECK" KELLY waves from atop a flagpole on a skyscraper in Manhattan in the late 1920s.

127

Frantic stock traders struggle to save their investments in October 1929, at the beginning of the 1929 STOCK MARKET CRASH.

THE PARTY'S OVER

The 1920s came in with a roar and ended with a crash. The crash came from the stock market, which fell to the floor just a few months before the decade ended. The spree was over. In place of "Ain't We Got Fun" Americans started singing "Brother, Can You Spare a Dime?"

The Great Depression was marked by massive unemployment, widespread business failure, homelessness, and even starvation. Down-and-out men sneaked rides on freight trains, traveling from town to town to look for work. Dust storms ravaged the Midwest, leading whole families to abandon their farms and take to the road.

On the surface, the trappings of the 1920s remained. The Chrysler Building stood tall and sparkly on the New York skyline, but inside were failing businesses and empty offices. The movies—now 100 percent talking—were more dazzling than ever. But outside the theaters and other city buildings, hungry people lined up for blocks, waiting for handouts of soup and bread. Jazz bands still played in the Cotton Club and Connie's Inn, but rich sophisticates no longer threw around their money and carelessly ordered champagne there. In many cases, even the rich had gone broke.

As the Depression ground on, people looked back on the high-rolling 1920s with great fondness. In his essay "Echoes of the Jazz Age," F. Scott Fitzgerald offered this

African American women show off the best of **FLAPPER FASHION** in Harlem in 1927.

assessment: "It was an age of miracles, it was an age of art, it was an age of excess, and it was an age of satire."

Throughout the twentieth century, the stories of flappers and speakeasies only improved with age. But through the long lens of many decades, it's easy to romanticize the 1920s. It was a great time for some, but many suffered during this decade. In some ways, society was ripped in pieces. Many Americans of the 1920s lashed out at immigrants, labor leaders, and anyone with radical political views. Many hated Catholics, as witnessed by the smear campaign against Al Smith during the 1928 presidential election. The Ku Klux Klan terrorized blacks during this era, and most blacks lived in poverty. Farmers also struggled just to feed their families. Religious conservatives were distraught during the 1920s. They believed the jazz music, new women, and illegal drinking of the big city signaled the end of moral, values-based society.

Setting aside this turmoil, people in the twenty-first century can still have a lot of fun learning about the twenties. Novels such as *The Beautiful and Damned* and *Babbitt* offer fascinating insights into 1920s high society and the more typical person on the street. Movies such as *Safety Last* (1923) show us wide-eyed Americans trying to make sense of a new, speeded-up world. The popular music of the 1920s—from "Fascinating Rhythm" to "West End Blues"—is some of the greatest of all time.

The *Brooklyn Daily Eagle* announces **THE WALL STREET CRASH OF OCTOBER 24, 1929.**

History repeats itself. In the early 2000s, the stock market climbed higher and higher. Some investors made big fortunes. Then, in late 2008, the stock market tumbled. It didn't crash quite as dramatically as it did in 1929, but the big drop reminded people of those dark days. Government leaders went back and studied 1929. They tried to create new policies, to make sure that the 2008 crash didn't lead to another Great Depression. As this event shows, we can learn a lot from history, and the 1920s are a great place to start learning.

1920

- Prohibition goes into effect.
- Babe Ruth begins his first season with the New York Yankees.
- The League of Women Voters is founded.
- For the first time, all U.S. women are eligible to vote in the presidential election.
- Presidential election returns are broadcast on radio for the first time.
- Warren G. Harding wins the U.S. presidency.

1921

- Italian immigrants and anarchists Nicola Sacco and Bartolomeo Vanzetti go on trial for murder.
- Langston Hughes writes "Weary Blues."
- Rudolph Valentino stars in *The Sheik*.
- The first Miss America contest takes place in Atlantic City, New Jersey.
- Jack Dempsey defends his heavyweight title against Georges Carpentier (in the first boxing match ever broadcast on radio).

1922

- The Florida land rush begins.
- F. Scott Fitzgerald publishes *Tales of the Jazz Age*.
- Sinclair Lewis publishes *Babbitt*.
- *Readers' Digest* magazine is founded.
- Americans go crazy for ancient Egypt after the discovery of King Tut's tomb.

1923

- Calvin Coolidge becomes president after Warren Harding dies in office.
- Harold Lloyd stars in *Safety Last*.
- Colleen Moore stars in *Flaming Youth*.
- The Charleston debuts in the Broadway show *Runnin' Wild*.
- Yankee Stadium opens in New York.

1924

- Congress passes the National Origins Act, severely restricting immigration into the United States for all but northern Europeans.
- Calvin Coolidge is elected to his first full term as president.
- Aimee Semple McPherson creates a radio station to preach her Foursquare Gospel.
- *Lady, Be Good* opens on Broadway.
- George Gershwin writes *Rhapsody in Blue*.
- Louis Armstrong joins the Fletcher Henderson Orchestra in New York.
- Alvin "Shipwreck" Kelly kicks off the flagpole-sitting craze.

1925

- Twenty-five thousand Ku Klux Klan members parade down Pennsylvania Avenue in Washington, D.C.
- John Scopes goes on trial for teaching evolution in his high school biology class in Dayton, Tennessee.
- Harold Ross founds the *New Yorker* magazine.
- Bell Telephone devises the Vitaphone system for sound movies.
- Red Grange joins the Chicago Bears.

1926

- Mae West is arrested for promoting indecency in her play *Sex*.
- Gertrude Ederle swims the English Channel in record time.
- Jack Dempsey loses his heavyweight title to Gene Tunney.
- The National Broadcasting Company is founded.
- *The General*, starring Buster Keaton, plays on movie screens.

1927

- A flood on the Mississippi River leaves about one thousand dead and seven hundred thousand homeless.
- Charles Lindbergh becomes the first person to fly solo across the Atlantic Ocean.
- *Show Boat* opens on Broadway.
- *It*, starring Clara Bow, plays in movie theaters.
- *The Jazz Singer*, the first movie with spoken dialogue, plays in movie theaters.
- Babe Ruth hits a record sixty home runs in a season.

1928

- The United States signs the Kellogg-Briand Pact, an international treaty condemning war.
- Herbert Hoover wins the presidency, beating Al Smith in a landslide.
- The *National Dance Barn* radio show becomes the *Grand Ole Opry*.
- Peter Pan peanut butter arrives on store shelves.
- George Gershwin writes *An American in Paris*.

1929

- In the Saint Valentine's Day Massacre in Chicago, members of Al Capone's gang gun down members of Bugs Moran's gang.
- The Chrysler Building opens in New York.
- The Museum of Modern Art opens in New York.
- The Academy of Motion Picture Arts and Sciences hands out its first awards for achievement in acting and filmmaking.
- The stock market crashes, beginning the Great Depression.

SOURCE NOTES

9   Neal Bascomb, *Higher: A Historic Race to the Sky and the Making of a City* (New York: Doubleday, 2003), 12.

13   Nathan Miller, *New World Coming: The 1920s and the Making of Modern America* (New York: Da Capo Press, 2003), 83.

13   Ibid., 73.

14   Carrie Chapman Catt, "Mrs. Catt on the Election,"*New York Times*,November21,1920, http://query.nytimes.com/mem/archive -free/pdf?res=9B01EED71F3DE533A25 752C2A9679D946195D6CF (August 20, 2008).

14   Ibid.

15   Edward Behr, *Prohibition: Thirteen Years That Changed America* (New York: Arcade Publishing, 1996), 113.

15   Ibid.

18   Lynn Dumenil, *Modern Temper: American Culture and Society in the 1920s* (New York: Hill and Wang, 1995), 225.

19   *The Jazz Age*, DVD (Newton, NJ: Shanachie Entertainment Corporation, 2003).

20   Miller, *New World Coming*, 123.

22   Cyndy Bittinger, "The Business of America Is Business?" *Calvin Coolidge Memorial Foundation*, 2008, http://www.calvin-coolidge .org/html/the_business_of_america_is _bus.html (January 7, 2009).

23   Calvin Coolidge Memorial Foundation, "The Homestead," *Calvin Coolidge Memorial Foundation*, 2008, http://www.calvin-coolidge .org/html/the_homestead.html (January 7, 2009).

23   Behr, *Prohibition*, 226.

24   Robert A. Slayton, *Empire Statesman: The Rise and Redemption of Al Smith* (New York: Free Press, 2001), 192.

24   T. H. Watkins, *The Hungry Years: A Narrative History of the Great Depression in America* (New York: Henry Holt and Company, 1999), 13.

27   Behr, *Prohibition*, 82–83.

28   Ibid., 150.

30   Behr, *Prohibition*, 78.

31   Marion Elizabeth Rodgers, ed., *The Impossible H. L. Mencken: A Selection of His Best Newspaper Stories* (New York: Anchor Books, 1991), 111.

33   Ibid.

34   F. Scott Fitzgerald, *The Beautiful and Damned* (New York: Charles Scribner's Sons, 1922), 388.

35   Miller, *New World Coming*, 298.

35   Behr, *Prohibition*, 226.

37   Sinclair Lewis, *Babbitt* (1922, repr., New York: Penguin Books, 1996), 3.

37   Ibid., 138.

40   AdClassix.com, "1927 Oldsmobile Six De-Luxe Coach," *AdClassix.com*, 2008, http:// www.adclassix.com/ads/27oldsmobile.htm (January 7, 2009).

41   Robert S. Lynd and Helen Merrell Lynd, *Middletown: A Study in Modern American Culture* (San Diego: Harcourt Brace and Company, 1929), 251.

41   Ibid., 46.

42   Miller, *New World Coming*, 328.

44   AdClassix.com, "1927 Frigidaire Refrigerator," *AdClassix.com*, 2008, http://www .adclassix.com/a3/27frigidairerefrigerator .htm (January 7, 2009).

45   Joshua Zeitz, *Flapper: A Madcap Story of Sex, Style, Celebrity, and the Women Who Made America Modern* (New York: Three Rivers Press, 2006), 66.

45   Miller, *New World Coming*, 151.

45   Zeitz, *Flapper*, 66.

45   Ibid., 200.

49   Bascomb, *Higher*, 80.

49   Rodgers, *Impossible H. L. Mencken*, 109.

50   Bascomb, *Higher*, 195.

50   Miller, *New World Coming*, 359.

51   Dumenil, *Modern Temper*, 60.

52   Bascomb, *Higher*, 80.

52   Miller, *New World Coming*, 282.

55   Bascomb, *Higher*, 156.

55   Miller, *New World Coming*, 370.

56   Ibid., 373.

59   Dumenil, *Modern Temper*, 134.

61   Angela Latham, *Posing a Threat: Flappers, Chorus Girls, and Other Brazen Performers of the American 1920s* (Hanover, NH: University Press of New England, 2000), 90.

63   Ibid., 48.

64   Dumenil, *Modern Temper*, 131.

65   Ibid., 187.

79   Robert E. Drennan, ed., *The Algonquin Wits*

(New York: Citadel Press, 1968), 116.

83 Thomas Kunkel, *Genius in Disguise: Harold Ross of the New Yorker* (New York: Random House, 1995), 93–94.

86 Robert Hughes, *American Visions: The Epic History of Art in America* (New York: Alfred A. Knopf, 1997), 337.

90 Abraham A. Davidson, *Early American Art* (New York: Harper and Row, 1981), 202.

91 Latham, *Posing a Threat*, 20.

94 Emily Post, *Etiquette in Society, in Business, in Politics and at Home* (New York: Funk and Wagnalls Company, 1922), http://www.gutenberg.org/files/14314/14314-h/14314-h.htm#Page_617 (January 7, 2009).

94 David E. Kyvig, *Daily Life in the United States, 1920–1940: How Americans Lived through the "Roaring Twenties" and the Great Depression* (Chicago: Ivan R. Dee, 2002), 122.

99 Zeitz, *Flapper*, 262

101 Dumenil, *Modern Temper*, 134.

101 Miller, *New World Coming*, 242.

107 *Jazz: A Film by Ken Burns*. Episode 2: "The Gift," DVD (Alexandria, VA: PBS Paramount, 2004).

109 Red Hot Jazz, "Duke Ellington and His Cotton Club Orchestra," *Red Hot Jazz*, 2008, http://www.redhotjazz.com/dukecco.html (January 7, 2009).

110 *Jazz*, "The Gift," DVD.

116 Hal Bock, "Yankee Stadium: Remembering a Baseball Cathedral," *USA Today*, July 3, 2008, http://www.usatoday.com/sports/baseball/2008-07-03-3198094899_x.htm (January 7, 2009).

130 Edmund Wilson, ed., *The Crack-Up* (New York: New Directions, 1945), 14.

SELECTED BIBLIOGRAPHY

Bascomb, Neal. *Higher: A Historic Race to the Sky and the Making of a City*. New York: Doubleday, 2003.
In the 1920s, New York City boomed and skyscrapers sprung up from the city sidewalks. This book tells the fascinating story of two architects who raced to build the city's tallest building. In describing the race, Bascomb also paints a vivid picture of 1920s New York.

Behr, Edward. *Prohibition: Thirteen Years That Changed America*. New York: Arcade Publishing, 1996.
Less than an hour after Prohibition took effect on January 17, 1920, six armed men stole one hundred thousand dollars worth of whiskey in Chicago. An era of lawbreaking, corruption, carousing, and gangsterism had begun. In this fact-filled book, Behr shows how Prohibition affected American society at nearly every level.

Dumenil, Lynn. *Modern Temper: American Culture and Society in the 1920s*. New York: Hill and Wang, 1995.
Dumenil looks beyond Jazz Age glamour to examine trends in 1920s society, including consumerism, modernism, and liberalism.

Glennon, Lorraine, ed. *Our Times: The Illustrated History of the 20th Century*. Atlanta: Turner Publishing, 1995.
This terrific book examines the twentieth century year by year, with coverage of art, politics, sports, and entertainment. Colorful photographs and illustrations bring history to life.

Hughes, Robert. *American Visions: The Epic History of Art in America*. New York: Alfred A. Knopf, 1997.
This brilliant book examines American history by exploring American art and architecture. Hughes discusses the American modernists of the 1920s, art deco, skyscrapers, and more.

The Jazz Age. DVD. Newton, NJ: Shanachie Entertainment Corporation, 2003.
Produced in 1956, this documentary takes a clear-eyed look at 1920s America—from politics to the new woman. The film features archival footage and a great 1920s sound track.

Kyvig, David E. *Daily Life in the United States, 1920–1940: How Americans Lived through the "Roaring Twenties" and the Great Depression*. Chicago: Ivan R. Dee, 2002.
In the 1920s, with new conveniences such as radio, cars, and electrical appliances, American life speeded up. In the following decade, the nation fell headfirst into the Great Depression. Kyvig examines how Americans adjusted to changes in society, economy, and daily life in both decades.

Latham, Angela. *Posing a Threat: Flappers, Chorus Girls, and Other Brazen Performers of the American 1920s*. Hanover, NH: University Press of New England, 2000.
When women switched from high-collared, long-skirted Victorian dress to skimpy flapper costumes, many Americans were shocked. Latham, a theater historian, explores how changing women's fashions reflected changing morality in 1920s society.

Lynd, Robert S., and Helen Merrell Lynd. *Middletown: A Study in Modern American Culture*. San Diego: Harcourt Brace and Company, 1929.
In the late 1920s, sociologists Robert and Helen Lynd conducted extensive studies and interviews in Muncie, Indiana, which they labeled Middletown—the typical U.S. city. The resulting book offers a fascinating window into 1920s society, culture, and family life.

Miller, Nathan. *New World Coming: The 1920s and the Making of Modern America*. New York: Da Capo Press, 2003.
Miller paints a vivid picture of 1920s America—a world filled with flappers and gangsters, jazz music and talking pictures, booming business, and the high-flying stock market.

Rodgers, Marion Elizabeth, ed. *The Impossible H. L. Mencken: A Selection of His Best Newspaper Stories*. New York: Anchor Books, 1991.
Opinionated and outspoken, *Baltimore Evening Sun* columnist H. L. Mencken remarked on key events and figures of the 1920s, everything from President Warren Harding to the Scopes trial to the Ku Klux Klan. His top newspaper columns are reprinted here.

Slayton, Robert A. *Empire Statesman: The Rise and Redemption of Al Smith*. New York: Free Press, 2001.
This detailed biography examines New York politician Al Smith—much beloved by his fellow New Yorkers. When Smith ran for president, however, he faced a slew of ugly, anti-Catholic propaganda. Most historians believe that religious prejudice led to Smith's landslide defeat at the polls.

TO LEARN MORE

Books

Feldman, Ruth Tenzer. *Calvin Coolidge*. Minneapolis: Twenty-First Century Books, 2007.
During the presidency of Calvin Coolidge, the United States prospered as it never had before. Industry boomed and the stock market climbed high. But during this era of mechanization and commercialism, Coolidge remained an old-fashioned, small-town American. This book tells his story.

Gourley, Catherine. *Flappers and the New American Woman: Perceptions of Women from 1918 through the 1920s*. Minneapolis: Twenty-First Century Books, 2008.
In this star-reviewed title, Gourley examines American women via media images. She combs through magazines, advertisements, films, and other media of the 1920s to see how U.S. society viewed women and how women viewed themselves.

Hill, Laban Carrick. *Harlem Stomp! A Cultural History of the Harlem Renaissance*. New York: Little, Brown Young Readers, 2009.
Harlem in the 1920s was home to African American writers, artists, and musicians. This book explores the cultural explosion that came to be called the Harlem Renaissance.

Lazo, Caroline Evensen. *F. Scott Fitzgerald*. Minneapolis: Twenty-First Century Books, 2003.
In his novels and short stories, Fitzgerald captured the spirit of the Jazz Age—from the flappers to the speakeasies to the Lost Generation. In this biography, Lazo explores Fitzgerald's life and work.

Lieurance, Suzanne. *The Prohibition Era in American History*. Berkeley Heights, NJ: Enslow Publishers, 2003.
The Prohibition amendment, which outlawed the manufacture and sale of liquor in the United States, ushered in an era of lawlessness—some of it harmless and some of it deadly. This book examines Prohibition and its effects on U.S. society.

McDonough, Yona Zeblis. *Who Was Louis Armstrong?* New York: Grosset and Dunlap, 2004.
This lushly illustrated biography chronicles the life of horn player Louis Armstrong, a name synonymous with 1920s jazz.

Ruth, Amy. *Herbert Hoover*. Minneapolis: Twenty-First Century Books, 2004.
Herbert Hoover was a skilled administrator who held several top government positions before being elected U.S. president in 1928. The stock market crashed shortly into his first term, forever linking Hoover's name with the Great Depression. This biography examines his triumphs as well as his failures.

Websites

American Cultural History: The Twentieth Century
http://kclibrary.lonestar.edu/decades.html
This site from the Lone Star College-Kingwood College Library in Texas provides useful overviews of each decade of U.S. cultural history in the twentieth century.

Duke Ellington
http://www.dukeellington.com
Duke Ellington was the greatest jazz bandleader of the 1920s. This official site from the Ellington estate offers film and music clips, photos, a complete Ellington discography, and much more.

Lindbergh
http://www.pbs.org/wgbh/amex/lindbergh/
This website, a companion to the PBS television show of the same name, gives a detailed look at "Lucky Lindy" and his 1927 solo flight across the Atlantic Ocean. The site includes a timeline, maps, and more.

Monkey Trial: An All-Out War Between Science and Religion
http://www.pbs.org/wgbh/amex/monkeytrial/
This website accompanies the PBS film of the same name, part of the acclaimed *American Experience* series. The site includes contemporary political cartoons, trial transcripts, political and cultural background, and more.

Films

F. Scott Fitzgerald: Winter Dreams. Alexandria, VA: PBS, 2001.
Part of the *American Masters* series, this documentary examines Fitzgerald's life and literary legacy.

Jazz: A Film by Ken Burns. DVD. Alexandria, VA: PBS Paramount, 2004.
This award-winning ten-part film traces the history of jazz music in the United States. Episodes 2 and 3 deal specifically with the 1920s, with detailed information on Louis Armstrong, Duke Ellington, Bix Beiderbecke, Bessie Smith, and other artists. The films include archival footage from the Cotton Club and other speakeasies, as well historic still photographs and original recordings.

Books

Fitzgerald, F. Scott. *The Great Gatsby*. 1925. Reprint, New York: Simon and Schuster, 1995.
Considered Fitzgerald's greatest work, *The Great Gatsby* tells the tale of the rich and beautiful in Jazz Age America via the lives of young businessman Nick Carraway, the wealthy and mysterious Jay Gatsby, and the enticing Daisy Buchanan.

Hurston, Zora Neale. *The Complete Stories*. New York: HarperCollins, 1995.
This collection of Hurston's short stories includes eight stories published in the 1920s, as well as later publications and unpublished work.

Lewis, Sinclair. *Babbitt*. 1922. Reprint, New York: Penguin Books, 1996.
Lewis's keen satire exposes the superficiality and hypocrisy of middle-class America through the character of George Babbitt, a blowhard real estate dealer in Zenith, Ohio.

Parker, Dorothy. *The Portable Dorothy Parker*. New York: Penguin Classics, 2006.
This collection showcases Parker's sharp wit and broad interests in a selection of her poems, articles, short stories, political essays, and letters from the 1920s on.

Toomer, Jean. *Cane*. 1923. Reprint, New York: Modern Library, 1994.
This classic of the Harlem Renaissance combines prose, poetry, and dialogue to paint a vivid picture of the African American experience in the early twentieth century.

Movies

The Coconuts. DVD. Chatsworth, CA: Image Entertainment, 1998.
The Marx Brothers took their stage act to the big screen in 1929. In this classic comedy (with music by Irving Berlin), Groucho Marx plays a Florida hotel owner who desperately needs cash during the Florida land boom. When brothers Chico and Harpo Marx get involved, hilarity ensures.

The Harold Lloyd Comedy Collection. DVD. New York: New Line Home Video, 2005.
This seven-disc collection includes almost all Lloyd's feature-length films and shorts, including *The Freshman*, *Speedy*, and the fabulous *Safety Last*.

It. DVD. New York: Kino International, 2002.
Clara Bow defines the image of the flapper in this 1927 silent classic. Bow plays a shopgirl who sets out to win her millionaire boss's heart.

The Sheik/The Son of the Sheik. DVD. Chatsworth, CA: Image Entertainment, 2002.
In the 1921 silent classic *The Sheik,* an Arab sheik (Rudolph Valentino) kidnaps a British beauty and carries her off to his desert home. The film established Valentino as the consummate screen lover. He reprised his role (playing both the sheik and his son) in *The Son of the Sheik* (1926).

1920s ACTIVITY

Identify six to ten things in your family or community history that relate to the 1920s. (To start, consider family antiques or collections, your house or buildings in your neighborhood, favorite movies, books, songs, and places you've visited.) Use photographs, mementos, and words to create a print or computer scrapbook of your 1920s connections.

143

ABOUT THE AUTHORS

Based in California, Edmund Lindop wrote several books for the Presidents Who Dared series as well as several of the titles in The Decades of Twentieth-Century America series.

Margaret J. Goldstein was born in Detroit and graduated from the University of Michigan. She is an editor and author for young readers. She lives in Santa Fe, New Mexico.

PHOTO ACKNOWLEDGMENTS

The images in this book are used with the permission of: All page backgrounds: © iStockphoto.com/ Cheryl Graham; © Hulton Archive/Getty Images, pp. 3, 16, 33, 34, 53, 56, 61, 68, 74, 112–113; Library of Congress, pp. 4–5 (LC-USZ62-107834), 7 (LC-USZ62-99824), 8–9 (LC-USZ62-95475), 13 (ppmsc 03671), 15 (LC-DIG-hec-19651), 21 (LC-USZ62-110625), 22 (LC-DIG-npcc-26147), 22–23 (LC-DIG-ggbain-37230), 24 (LC-USZ62-17145), 28 (LC-USZ62-123257), 29 (LC-USZ62-93270), 30–31 (LC-USZ62-42087), 42 (LC-USZ62-22847), 44 (LC-USZ62-109738), 47 (LC-USZ62-97394), 70 (LC-USZ61-1854), 73 (LC-USZ62-111409), 77 (LC-USZ62-84002), 103 (LC-DIG-ppmsc-03674), 108 (LC-USZ62-54141), 116–117 (LC-DIG-npcc-04037), 120 (LC-DIG-npcc-15254), 124 (LC-USZ62-94046), 125 (LC-DIG-npcc-02710), 126 (LC-DIG-npcc-11609), 140 (left) (LC-DIG-npcc-04037), 140 (middle) (LC-USZ62-123257); © Frank Driggs Collection/Hulton Archive/Getty Images, pp. 6, 69, 106–107, 110, 140 (right); Minnesota Historical Society, pp. 10–11; AP Photo, pp. 12, 25, 26, 41, 48, 55, 64, 65, 66, 78, 79, 102, 118–119, 120, 121, 127; © Bettmann/CORBIS, pp. 14, 81; From the Collections of The Henry Ford (THF22022), p. 17; AP Photo/File, pp. 18, 105; © P. L. Sperr/Hulton Archive/Getty Images, p. 19; © Topical Press Agency/Hulton Archive/Getty Images, pp. 20, 62; © National Archives/Newsmakers/Getty Images, p. 31 (left); © Popperfoto/Getty Images, p. 31 (right); © Underwood Photo Archives/SuperStock, p. 32; © Chicago History Museum/Hulton Archive/Getty Images, p. 35; © General Photographic Agency/Hulton Archive/Getty Images, pp. 36–37, 39, 71, 93; © SuperStock, Inc./SuperStock, p. 38; Charles W. Cushman Collection, Indiana University Archives (P10099, original image is color), pp. 40–41; © Schenectady Museum; Hall of Electrical History Foundation/CORBIS, p. 43; © McNEIL-PPC, Inc. 2009, Advertisement © 1920s. Used by permission., p. 45; © H. Armstrong Roberts/ Retrofile/Getty Images, p. 46; © Culver Pictures, Inc./SuperStock, p. 50; © A. E. French/Hulton Archive/ Getty Images, p. 51; © FPG/Hulton Archive/Getty Images, pp. 52, 67, 131; © Vintage Images/Hulton Archive/Getty Images, p. 54; The Granger Collection, New York, pp. 58–59, 82, 88, 91, 130; © American Stock/Hulton Archive/Getty Images, p. 60; Famous Players/Paramount/The Kobal Collection, p. 63; © Pro Football Hall of Fame/NFL/Getty Images, p. 72; © New York Times Co./Hulton Archive/Getty Images, p. 76; © E. O. Hoppe/Mansell/Time & Life Pictures/Getty Images, p. 80; Digital Image © The Museum of Modern Art/Licensed by SCALA/Art Resource, NY, p. 84; © The Newark Museum/Art Resource, NY, p. 86; © 2009 Man Ray Trust/Artists Rights Society (ARS), NY/ADAGP, Paris. Image provided by: © Man Ray Trust/ ADAGP – ARS/Telimage – 2009, p. 87; © Danny Moloshok/Reuters/CORBIS, p. 89; © Caufield & Shook/ FPG/Hulton Archive/Getty Images, p. 90; © MPI/Hulton Archive/Getty Images, p. 92; © Bob Thomas/ Popperfoto/Getty Images, p. 94; © Edwin Levick/Hulton Archive/Getty Images, p. 95; The Art Archive/ Culver Pictures, pp. 96–97; The Art Archive/Museum of the City of New York/MCNY79, p. 98; United Artists/ The Kobal Collection, p. 99; Hal Roach/Pathe Exchange/The Kobal Collection/Kornman, Gene, pp. 100–101; Paramount/The Kobal Collection, p. 101; Warner Bros/The Kobal Collection, p. 104; © Gilles Petard/ Redferns/Getty Images, p. 109; © Lebrecht Music and Arts Photo Library/Alamy, p. 111; © Underwood & Underwood/CORBIS, p. 112; © Fox Photos/Hulton Archive/Getty Images, p. 114; © Gaston Paris/Roger Viollet/Getty Images, p. 115; © Mark Rucker/Transcendental Graphics/Getty Images, p. 118; AP Photo/ NYRA, p. 123; © OFF/AFP/Getty Images, pp. 128–129.

Front Cover: © General Photographic Agency/Hulton Archive/Getty Images (top left); © Frank Driggs Collection/Hulton Archive/Getty Images (top right); © Library of Congress/Hulton Archive/Getty Images (bottom left); Library of Congress (LC-USZ62-12142) (bottom right).